I wish I had read this book thirty [...] dous encouragement and motivati [...] one might be in, as a Christian, an [...] the light of Christ shine through y [...] handbook for sharing the love of C. [...] member, friend, parishioner, or stranger. I heartily recommend what Pastor Espinosa has to say in this book about *Faith That Engages the Culture*.

REV. PETER LANGE,
FIRST VICE-PRESIDENT, LCMS

Evangelism texts are aplenty, and they run the gamut from books focused on asking good questions to texts that speak about establishing key friendships with nonbelievers—and all topics in between. Yet Dr. Espinosa's work stands out as unique among them all for three specific reasons: (1) he approaches the topic through a distinctly Lutheran theological lens, bringing both Scripture and the Lutheran Confessions to the task of evangelism; (2) he bridges the divide between those who seek to engage intellectually and those who desire to engage relationally in this work; and (3) he brings into the conversation a divergent group of voices to speak on the contextual nature of witnessing. I hope that many will "read, learn, inwardly digest, and outwardly practice" a *Faith That Engages the Culture*.

REV. JONATHAN B. RUEHS,
ASSISTANT PROFESSOR OF THEOLOGY AND DIRECTOR OF THE
CENTER FOR CHURCH LEADERSHIP, CONCORDIA UNIVERSITY, IRVINE

Faith That Engages the Culture comes in an age of cultural contradictions. Pastor Espinosa first lays out a thesis for the reader using the very foundations of the Christian faith: Scripture, the Lutheran Confessions, and theological writings. After clearly defining these building blocks, he masterfully crafts them together through helpful and practical scenarios of God's people who have encountered specific issues both in the world and their Christian faith. These guides are not only useful in bringing those around you the saving Gospel but are also wise words in which each reader can find faith-strengthening truth.

CRYSTEN SANCHEZ,
EVENTS EXECUTIVE, HIGHER THINGS, INC.

Acts 17

Faith That Engages the Culture is a field manual for Christian laity who live and work on the cultural front lines and desperately need pastoral guidance. Dr. Espinosa shows that the unchanging truths of Scripture, as taught in Luther's Small Catechism, are the Christian's guide for engaging a culture that rejects the truth of God's Word in favor of individualism, relativism, and skepticism. His approach is sensitive, focusing on perspective, people, and place while presenting an uncompromising confession of God's Word. Always, the focus remains on the center of Scripture, the crucified and risen Jesus Christ.

REV. TODD WILKEN,
HOST, ISSUES, ETC.

Espinosa's work is magisterial in its breadth and boldness. He charts a new course for apologetics and evangelization that is moored in a dialogical methodology that opens up engagement. The tools to open up such engagement are active listening and humility. Accordingly, both theology and science must demonstrate humility by respecting their inherent limitations. Apologetics, then, is not an intellectual blood sport; it is not about winning arguments. Apologetics certainly cannot be a monologue—a one-way, agenda-laden conversation derived from an era that was blatantly imperial, oppressive, and certainly monological. Espinosa's understanding of apologetics in this book speaks to us living in a postcolonial world. Espinosa avers that opening up a dialogical approach entails having a proper relationship between Law and Gospel. The proper application of the Law entails sensitivity, looking beyond surface sins to the greater disease that we all share—a disease that fulminates in an array of emotions that Christ alone can quell and heal.

REV. TIMOTHY L. SEALS, PHD,
SENIOR PASTOR OF ST. LUKE LUTHERAN CHURCH,
CLAREMONT, CALIFORNIA

FAITH
THAT
ENGAGES
THE
CULTURE

ALFONSO ESPINOSA

CONCORDIA PUBLISHING HOUSE · SAINT LOUIS

Published by Concordia Publishing House
3558 S. Jefferson Avenue, St. Louis, MO 63118-3968
1-800-325-3040 • cph.org

Manufactured in the United States of America

1 2 3 4 5 6 7 8 9 10   30 29 28 27 26 25 24 23 22 21

DEDICATION

To Ellie, Noah, Natalie, Emily, Lizzy, Isaiah,
and James in the womb.
Like children, grandchildren are also a heritage
and gift from the Lord!
—and—

To Rev. Mark Jasa, evangelist of the Lord Jesus Christ,
my colleague, friend, and brother in Christ.
—and—

To Rev. Paul T. McCain, now with the Lord in heaven,
who greatly encouraged me to write this book
in service to God's redeemed and to the glory
of Jesus Christ.

ACKNOWLEDGMENTS

I would like to thank the servants of God who have helped form and teach me. I thank my first LCMS pastor, Rev. John A. Miller III, the first one who made the Gospel clear to me. He taught me that there is no engagement if we are not full of thanksgiving for what Christ has done for us. That's why he said, "Evangelism is caught, not taught." And while my view is now a combination of the two, I think that at the end of the day my old pastor had the right emphasis. When I was a student at Christ College Irvine (now Concordia University, Irvine), Professor Dale Hartmann and the late Rev. Dr. Charles Manske equipped and inspired me to engage. As a seminarian, I had a chance to sit down with Rev. Ken Behnken, who was the mission executive for the Pacific Southwest District of The Lutheran Church—Missouri Synod at the time. I asked him about the best way to learn evangelization. That was about thirty-two years ago and turned out to be the shortest interview I ever conducted. He said, "Do it!" I've never forgotten the bottom line for engagement! I am also grateful for Rev. George Mather, a tremendously gifted evangelist. His prescription is also straightforward: "Just love people and point them to Jesus!" George is an inspiration. I also wish to thank my father-confessor, Rev. Robert Dargatz, especially as he cared for me while I wrote the final manuscript through February of 2020. He has kept pointing *me* to Jesus.

I also want to thank my amazing congregation: Saint Paul's Lutheran Church of Irvine, California. This congregation is my little paradise on earth because these Christians love Christ's Word and Sacraments. I am also indebted to my colleagues Rev. Steven Mueller and Rev. A. J. Espinosa who cover me when I'm away.

Closer to home, I wish to thank my parishioner Ms. Cindy Ackley. While I was holed up in my study for a month, she assisted my wife, Traci, around the house, and that is no small task at the Espinosa residence! I also want to thank my firstborn, my son Rev. A. J. Espinosa, ABD. For the last two and a half years, we have talked about various things related to this book on and off, and I'm sure he didn't realize how helpful he was, as he has grown to be an excellent theologian. Also, my second born, Mrs. Elizabeth Snyder—MA in clinical psychology—helped me tighten up my chapter on depression and is a great encourager. I also thank my daughters Christina and Esbeydi, whose bedrooms are adjacent to my study and had to tolerate their father up at all hours, and who literally brought me food.

As for directly touching my work in this book, I thank the phenomenal interviewees, specialists in the various fields addressed in this book:

Rev. Mark Jasa, who is the most gifted evangelist I know: Sharing the Gospel

Dr. Roderick Soper and Dr. Gabriela Espinosa: Science

Dr. Russell Dawn and Dr. Paul Fick: Politics

Dr. Cari Chittick and Dr. Kristen Koenig: Personhood

Vicar Brian Barlow, Heather Ruesch, and two anonymous brothers in Christ: Sexuality

Dr. Paul Fick and Dr. Roberto Flores de Apodaca: Addiction

Dr. Shannon Gallina and Rev. Todd Peperkorn: Depression

Focusing on book production though, there were a few individuals whom I could not have done without. First, Mr. Brad Perry set up a new workstation for me. The extra-large monitor and the very comfortable new keyboard were a blessing! In addition, Mr. Todd Gallina was my designer and artist for the symbolism that solidified my conceptualizations for the *engagement triangle*. Also, Mrs. Denise Seaman was extremely important for this book, as she led the process to secure permissions for the various sources referenced in this book—an arduous task requiring organization and people skills. And finally, Mrs. Kiu Geisler, who was a great help in preparing my footnotes per

Chicago Manual of Style standards *and* tracking and formatting the bibliography. In other words, I had a team sent from heaven for this book! I praise God for each and every one.

I cannot forget the people at Concordia Publishing House. I was privileged to work with the same team as before: Paul McCain, Scot Kinnaman, and Laura Lane are the folks who make visions that glorify God into reality. The LCMS is extremely blessed to have these faithful servants of Christ.

Finally, I save the best for last just under the Lord Jesus, one who is His servant and the one who completes me: my wife, Traci Dawn. People have no idea how much she helps me. Not only does she care for me in such a complete way, but her fingerprints are all over this book. And in saving the best for last regarding her, *she* engages *me*. When I've needed to hear the sweet and empowering Gospel, she has reminded me of and proclaimed to me God's grace in Christ, and apart from this engagement, this book would not exist.

TABLE OF CONTENTS

FOREWORD

"This is eternal life, that they know You, the only true God, and Jesus Christ whom You have sent" (John 17:3). These words from our Lord's High Priestly Prayer kept going through my mind as I read this wonderful book on engaging others with the Gospel of Christ by Al Espinosa. As Christians who have been comforted and strengthened by our Savior's forgiveness and mercy, whose lives are lived by faith in the undeserved grace of God in Christ, we simply want others to know Him who gave His life for us. Pastor Espinosa has not written another how-to book on evangelism and outreach. Instead, this is a comforting homily for every Lutheran Christian and pastor not to be afraid to talk about their faith with others. It is what we do!

Don't let the title of this book scare you. This book is for every Christian. Engagement is very simply our calling not only to be students of the Scriptures but also of the people whom God has placed in our path and the culture in which we live. We do this so that we might faithfully engage others with the Gospel of Christ. Pastor Espinosa calls this a triangle of "perspective, people, and place." It is a handy pneumonic device, and it rings true. We do what we do as Christians in engaging the world around us because we love our Lord Jesus Christ and we love our fellow sinners for whom He shed His blood. Paul's words serve as the underlayment throughout the book: "I have become all things to all people, that by all means I might save some. I do it all for the sake of the gospel, that I may share with them in its blessings" (1 Corinthians 9:22–23).

It was near and dear to my heart that each chapter began with apt citations from the Small Catechism and the Lutheran Confessions. These were not perfunctory insertions but were foundational and interpretive for everything that followed. Pastor Espinosa repeatedly demonstrates the proper ministerial use of reason as he explores the topics of science, politics, and personhood in the culture around us and sexuality, addiction, and depression in the culture within us. While drawing upon experts in those fields, poignant case studies, and interviews, Pastor Espinosa always approaches each topic of engagement as a compassionate theologian and pastor. The Word of God and the Good News of God's love for the sinner always speak the final and definitive word.

When I read a theological work, I often go to the section that I believe will open a window into the mind and heart of the author. What does he believe? What makes him tick? Pastor Espinosa's exposition of 1 Peter 3:15 in chapter 4 is spot-on. "In your hearts honor Christ the Lord as holy, always being prepared to make a defense to anyone who asks you for a reason for the hope that is in you; yet do it with gentleness and respect." Often used as a proof text for Christian apologetics, Pastor Espinosa demonstrates that the apostle's words have everything to do with Christian vocation—the call to "proclaim the excellencies of Him who called [us] out of darkness into His marvelous light" (1 Peter 2:9). We are called to confess our faith in Christ and "make a defense" for the peculiar way we live as Christians. We don't just believe in Christ, but this faith in the love of God in Christ shapes the way we live in our calling as men and women, husbands and wives, parents and children, citizens and workers. Everything we are as Christians is shaped and ordered by the Gospel of God's unmerited mercy in Christ. This is often a trigger for those who do not know Christ: "Why do you love your wife like you do?" "Why do you care for people whom nobody else cares for?" "Why do you treat your boss with such respect; he doesn't deserve it!" Answer: "Because that is what my Lord Jesus did for me, and that is what He did for you!"

Al Espinosa is one of the most genuine, authentic Christian men I have ever known. Spend a long weekend in his home and parish and you will soon learn that he lives everything he talks about in this book. *Faith That Engages the Culture* is meticulously researched, authentically Lutheran, thoroughly biblical, yet down to earth and practical in every way. If you are a pastor, his guidance will give you invaluable insights into the kinds of conversations we are called to have when we hear confessions and comfort troubled souls. If you are a layperson, his wisdom and insights will teach you how to listen and confess Christ to those who do not know Him. And for all of us, he teaches us how to love our fellow sinners and not be afraid to give them Jesus. Thanks, Al! To God alone be the glory!

Rev. Peter C. Bender, pastor
Peace Lutheran Church
Director of the Concordia Catechetical Academy
Sussex, Wisconsin

PREFACE

The myriad approaches for sharing the Gospel (including the approach of not sharing it at all) has been one of those things that has never stopped bothering me. Along the way, I've come to find out that I am not the only Christian challenged by the question, "How does one share the Gospel?" This book was written to address this question.

As for verifying the *need* for this book, I've been confronted left and right. It is no secret how dramatically demographics in our culture are changing. More and more people in our country are without Christ. Many are unaware of the single most important message given to humanity, and many others think it irrelevant. The Church has never had such a serious need for her members to engage others with the saving Gospel of Jesus Christ. *Therefore, we need to be equipped on how to engage!*

I conducted a survey using this question: "Why do so many Christians find it difficult to engage people for the sake of sharing the Good News?"[1] There were many respondents, but three of them stood out for me:

> Sarah Gulseth contributed: "I think people just don't know what to say. We . . . are taught lots of great theological doctrine and all . . . these wonderful concepts about grace and faith and Baptism, but often we aren't taught how to simply explain all of those big concepts to someone who has zero background in Christianity and to whom those things are very foreign. Where do you begin the conversation? What do you say first to draw them in rather than confusing or belittling them?

---

[1] On May 17, 2019, on Facebook ("public" setting), I posted this along with a picture of my book *Faith That Sees through the Culture*. It received forty-nine comments, and of these, thirty-six were direct answers to the question. "Public" mode makes this accessible to everyone. All three "winners" mentioned in the book posted on May 17, 2019.

How do you say it so you can be empathetic to where they're coming from rather than coming off as rude or a know-it-all?"

Ashley Kmiec stated, "We can feel it is not our business to impose on others what we believe because society is becoming so diverse and versatile. It is no longer just the push of Christianity. There are so many other beliefs accepted. I also believe it's fear, and some feel uncomfortable or awkward. Many do not know how to even start sharing or where to begin, so out of fear of looking stupid or embarrassing themselves, they stay silent."

Finally, Sara Miller's feedback might be hard to accept, but it rings true: "If I'm honest, I think it's because I've made an idol of my own comfort. If I'm not ruffling anyone's feathers by talking about Jesus, faith, and sin, I grow complacent. Not to mention a conversation like that takes time, and I'm soooo busy. Not really but it's a lie I tell myself. Lord forgive me."

That last reason gets to *the* answer: we squirm out of witnessing on account of our sin. Christians are also sinners, and sinners don't want to share Christ. It's that simple and disturbingly sad at the same time. Note, however, Sara Miller's last words: they are in the form of a prayer asking for God's forgiveness. In Christ, we *are* forgiven! In response to this forgiveness, we owe it to God to share the Gospel in a way that is thoroughly biblical while emphasizing love toward the person we share with. Out of these concerns, I wrote this book—*Faith That Engages the Culture*.

INTRODUCTION

Faith Is a Gift

The terms in the title of this book are important to understand. The first word in the title is *faith*. This faith is the gift of God (Ephesians 2:8). It is the work of God in us (John 6:29). The Holy Spirit creates faith in us through the Word of Christ (Romans 10:17). This living faith has knowledge of the Word of God, accepts what God says as true, and trusts God in the way we live. This faith is always doing the good works that God has prepared in advance for His people to do (Ephesians 2:10). Faith leads us to constantly pray, constantly serve, constantly worship, and—this might be the part where Christians need the most encouragement—constantly *witness and engage*. This is what Christians are called to do: engage for the sake of the Gospel. We engage those for whom the Gospel is intended (which is everyone). Faith urges us to open our hearts and mouths in service and love so that people might come to know that Christ is for them, that the sweet, life-transforming Gospel is straight from God to them.

What Is Engagement?

The second word to understand is *engages*. Evangelism (sharing faith, witnessing for the Gospel, testifying to Christ), is *not* about us and our efforts. It is rather about *connecting* to the people who don't know the Gospel. *This is why engagement is emphasized throughout the book.* Christians are not sharing faith with robots, but with people for whom Christ gave His life—people created by God. People, all people, are precious to God. Regardless of how much one might be offended by another person, that person is as important to God as His most faithful and ardent Christian. This can be hard for a Christian to swallow, but it's true. Christ really did come for sinners, even those who bother us the most, even those who might tempt us to anger. The call to witness gets Christians off their high horses so they will love their neighbor instead of judging them.

Instead, the Christian is called to enter a loving, back-and-forth exchange. The Christian is called by God to get into the shoes of the unbeliever, sincerely becoming all things to all people (1 Corinthians 9:22). In this way, Christian engagement is not only a serious investment in the Word of God but *also* a serious investment in knowing and caring about the people with whom they share the Gospel. This process eliminates any conception of a one-way street: something the Christian does *toward* someone without the Gospel. Much to the contrary, the Christian realizes that without a real, mutual relationship, no one will care about how much you know until they know how much you care (to borrow from a well-known saying). This can't be faked. This can't be a strategic *move* for an ulterior motive. If Christians truly understand the Gospel means that God's heart is for all people to know His love for them in Christ, then Christians will not approach people in order to shove a message in their face, but rather the Christian will be driven to approach people out of love—not just love for God, but *love for the person whom they seek to engage.*

Where Does Engagement Happen?

We also need to have a clear understanding of *when* and *where* engagement occurs. It would be a mistake to limit engagement to knocking on doors to invite people to your local congregation, nor is it reduced to the person you might speak to on the train or in line for coffee. Engagement may occur and does occur in relationships you've had for years. It *might* happen with someone you meet one day and never see again; it could even happen online. But more often, the Lord works through the relationships you have in your various God-given vocations. God has a way of connecting you with people, and your circle of friends is probably broader than you realize: the mailman, the folks at that favorite restaurant you frequent, your brother or sister, your in-laws, co-workers, and friends. It might be your refinance guy, your hairstylist, your doctor, or your dentist. It might even be your spouse. Engagement happens with the people in your life. Never discount that it could *also* happen with a total stranger in a limited amount of time. But usually, the most meaningful engagements come with an investment in *relationship*, especially where there is a level of trust and mutual respect.

Culture

Finally, none of this happens in a vacuum. Any effort to bring the Gospel into a real engagement will be affected by external influences that come from the **culture** (the **place** in which engagement takes place). That is, when we engage, the two people involved are impacted by the culture to the extent that the culture itself affects moods, thoughts, values, what is considered real, the words we choose, and the actions we take. To be aware of the culture and cultural influence during engagement is invaluable, especially when appropriate adjustments can be made so that engagement is most fruitful. This does not mean that the Word of God is compromised. The Word is eternal and does not change. At the same time, how we *apply* the Word in a given engagement will consider the unique person and place.

Responses to Engagement

Nothing guarantees that we will be "successful" in an engagement. We can be 100 percent led by the Holy Spirit, and even experience real engagement, but never know what will result. In Acts 17, when St. Paul had concluded his engagement at the Areopagus, the Holy Scriptures record three basic responses: (1) Some mocked him; (2) others wanted to hear more but remained on the fence; and (3) others came to believe. In our culture today, we might add a fourth possible response: some don't care and will continue to view the Gospel as totally and utterly irrelevant. Keep in mind, however, that just because a person acts like they don't care doesn't mean they don't care. We must trust the Holy Spirit.

Rev. Mark Jasa tells the true story of his dialogues with an independently wealthy math professor at UCLA. From prior discussions with the professor, Pastor Jasa had already learned that the professor claimed he carried no guilt—evidently believing he had never done anything wrong—nor was he afraid of death. This is significant. In Pastor Jasa's work as an evangelist, he seeks to naturally lead people to their most basic and visceral needs: (1) dealing with their sense of guilt and shame (what C. S. Lewis refers to as the Law of Human Nature or the Rule of Right and Wrong having been violated);[2] and (2) facing something no one can solve: death. But again, the wealthy professor claimed no such dissonance or inkling that something was wrong.

As time passed, the math professor heard that Pastor Jasa had been engaging in the historical evidence for the resurrection of Jesus Christ from the dead. Evidently, the math professor was eager to see Pastor again. The professor came up to Rev. Jasa: "Hey, I heard you can prove that Jesus Christ rose from the dead!" Pastor Jasa replied, "It doesn't matter. Jesus has nothing to offer you." The professor—somewhat agitated—said, "Wait a minute; it's your job to make me a Christian!" Pastor Jasa was clear in his response: "No, no, no, my job is to give good news to bad people. There's nothing more for us to talk about." In other words, the professor had already made it known that he didn't need forgiveness nor rescue from death, so what did it matter if Christ was raised from the dead? When Pastor Jasa told me about this exchange, he reminded me of Luke 16:31: "[Jesus] said to him, 'If they do not hear Moses and the Prophets, neither will they be convinced if someone should rise from the dead.'"[3]

Christians Are Witnesses

We strive to do our part in the engagement, but we leave the results to the Holy Spirit. After all, we don't convert anyone; we are simply called to love people and share Jesus. The goal here is to do our part in the best way possible. We will leave the rest to God.

Sharing the Gospel one-on-one is not a church, religious, or spiritual specialization. It is rather to be viewed as a part of ordinary Christian life. When we treat sharing the Gospel as a natural and basic thing,

---

[2]   C. S. Lewis, *Mere Christianity: A Revised and Amplifed Edition, with a New Introduction, of the Three Books, Broadcast Talks, Christian Behaviour, and Beyond Personality* (New York: HarperCollins, 2001), 20.

[3]   Rev. Mark Jasa, interview by author, Long Beach, California, January 13, 2020.

then we are in the position to not only experience its personal benefits for our faith but more importantly, the person who receives the Gospel receives the greatest news anyone could possibly receive. Imagine that in the midst of the pandemic and in the worldwide scramble to find a vaccine, *you* miraculously come upon it. What do you do with it as people start to die around you? The answer is obvious: you share it.

The problem, however, is that even though Christians confess the truth of God's Word that people *need* the universal Gospel for the light of life instead of suffering the darkness of death, too many Christians don't back up their confession with their lives. Too often, Christians will not share the Gospel, because they are self-conscious about this or that. This is a selfish reaction in the face of the tremendous need of others to hear the witness of the Gospel.

The word *witness* itself is from the word *martyr*. The Ancient Church historian Eusebius wrote about the martyrs who gave up their lives as a witness to Christ in the Early Church. The martyrs got over themselves. They stopped playing that game of being self-conscious for every reason under the sun. Among other things, Eusebius wrote about the martyrs of the second century AD, and his testimony about them is amazing. The ancient Christian historian recorded the story of the martyr Blandina. The so-called "ingenious tormentors" tortured her, but they could not overcome her. There was nothing they could do—no matter how horrific—that could break her. "But this blessed saint, as a noble wrestler, in the midst of her confession itself received her strength . . . to repeat, 'I am a Christian.'"[4]

My wife, Traci, says, "I am a Christian," constantly as she cares for our grandchildren by witnessing to Jesus and telling them the Gospel. She sings them songs about the faith, she prays with them, and she reminds them that they are loved by Jesus. She is witnessing to them left and right. Yes, this is a far cry from what the martyrs did, but that doesn't mean that what my wife does is easy, nor does it mean that she doesn't allow a part of her life to die. Our adorable grandchildren are also a lot of work for her as she has mastered the art of multitasking.

---

4   C. F. Cruse, trans., *Eusebius' Ecclesiastical History: Complete and Unabridged,* New Updated Edition (Peabody, MA: Hendrickson, 1998), 148.

It takes a toll on her body, but she does it in love for our grandchildren. All Christians are witnesses and are at least little martyrs willing to let parts of themselves die (like their precious time, their ego, or their self-consciousness about witnessing). When these parts of us die, then God uses us to be His witnesses about the Good News of Jesus Christ for all people. But *how* do we witness? *How* do we engage?

An Organizing Matrix: Engagement Triangle

Sharing the Gospel—if done biblically and, as I will be arguing, if done naturally in relationships—will always consider these three things:

1. The **perspective**: The Word of God teaches us how to see engagement for the Gospel.

2. The **people**: Knowing ourselves and knowing the one with whom we are engaging.

3. The **place**: Understanding the cultural impact upon engagement.

Think of these three as forming a **triangle.** Furthermore, think of an equilateral triangle (as in a standard symbol of the Holy Trinity).

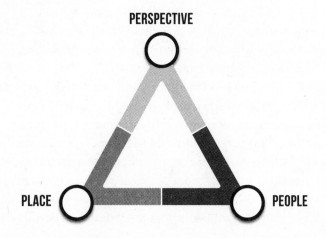

The top point is where we begin: the Word of God. This and this alone forms our **perspective**. The Word of God is truth, and it serves as an illuminating guide. It reveals the most important message one human being can share with another, as well as informs *how* that sharing should take place. If the sharing of the Gospel is happening in the right way, then no one is talking down to another, but there is a personal, respectful, and meaningful exchange between two equals. What should we call such an exchange? The word *engagement* reminds us that sharing the Gospel is never about a simple transfer of information from one person to another (one-directional), but a *back-and-forth* between two people in which *both* parties share what is on their hearts and minds. In this engagement, people connect face-to-face. The Christian includes within this engagement the Gospel, the single most important piece of any back-and-forth exchange.

Through this **perspective,** the **people** are carefully considered next. As you visualize the engagement triangle in front of you, look to the right side of the triangle and trace down to the bottom-right point. You've arrived at that which represents the **people** participating in the engagement: yourself and the one with whom you are engaging.

It might seem redundant and unnecessary, but the Christian who shares the Gospel must constantly consider *themselves*. What prejudices does the Christian bring while engaging whomever they're talking to? If the other person is of a different ethnicity, what beliefs does the Christian hold that might especially interfere with loving engagement? What if that other person identifies with a different religion or different political ideology? How will this affect the Christian sharing the Gospel? It is important to *know yourself.* Sometimes the greatest barriers between us and others are the ones we put up. We can get in the way of the Gospel we seek to share. Whatever negative reactions come up within us, we must eliminate them (*crucify the flesh!*) for the sake of constructive engagement. Apply God's Word to the temptation to remain quiet or to talk too much: "And those who belong to Christ Jesus have crucified the flesh with its passions and desires" (Galatians 5:24). Open your ears to listen and your mouth to speak as you reject the tendency to avoid real engagement for the Gospel.

In addition, the other person must be considered to the extent that an honest effort is made to get into their shoes. God calls His people to love Him, and then He calls His people to love others (Matthew 22:37–39; 1 John 4:20). If engagement is going to be a good thing and something blessed with God's presence and power, then the Christian must *love* the person they're engaging with. To love another person is to take genuine interest in them, to learn about their lives, and to respect them enough to shut our mouths so that we may listen. We should take a real interest and ask sincere questions. We should look for ways to love them as we get to know them. What an honor this is, to love someone who is loved by God!

Finally, travel from the bottom-right point (**people**) to the bottom-left point of the triangle. We arrive at **place**. The place is the culture, and the culture impacts everything else we've discussed up to this point. Culture consists of the man-made influences from the world, which contribute to the formation of a person's identifiable artifacts, words, behaviors, values, beliefs, and what they consider to be real. At the center of any person will be their ultimate allegiance or that which they live for. All these join forces to lead the person to live a certain way. If we ever stand a chance to effectively engage people, then we must know how the place in which they live impacts their formation as a person. There is, of course, an overarching culture in the United States, but there are also many subcultures. Because these subcultures or immediate places are often most influential upon the way people think and live, it is in the Christian's best interest to learn about these places for the sake of engagement for the Gospel.

What happens next with the engagement triangle? During the engagement, it repeats. From the bottom-left point of **place**, we run up the left side, back to the first point of **perspective** on top of the triangle. *We always return to our anchor and guide: the Word of God.* As the engagement continues, it is God's Word that keeps us focused and on track.

When we *are* focused and on track, then we get to the Gospel that gets us right with God and is totally and completely free, universal, unconditional, and 100 percent true. Rev. Mark Jasa, a gifted evangelist, helps us know the powerful yet profound simplicity of the Gospel. He offers these *three Gospel questions*:

1. Who did Jesus die for?[5]

2. How many sins did He pay for?

3. Which one of your sins did Jesus forget to pay for?[6]

Pastor Jasa's goal in his engagement with people is for them to get to the point of being able to answer each of the three questions on their own aloud while he engages them. He wants to hear them give the three answers: (1) All people! (2) All of them! (3) None of them! This is the outrageous Gospel that offends anyone who thinks that the key to being set free from guilt, shame, and death is to try harder, serving their own pride and ego to find a way to fix themselves. But for anyone who has tried and failed, and who knows they need help, the Gospel is beyond sweet.

---

[5] Some would say that by jumping into what seems a pure Gospel statement, we have left out the Law. This is inaccurate. The first statement, "Who did Jesus die for?" includes the Law. Why did Jesus have to die to begin with? Because all people are sinners and judged by God. So, *depending on where the person is at,* this first question may be a Law statement that transitions to the Gospel, or if the Holy Spirit has already convicted the person, then it is direct Gospel.

[6] Jasa, interview.

PART I:

ENGAGEMENT

TRIANGLE

EXPLAINED

CHAPTER 1:
ENGAGEMENT'S PERSPECTIVE
(LAW AND GOSPEL)

The Catechism Teaches the Two Ways of God's Word

Section 4 of Luther's Small Catechism consists of "Christian Questions with Their Answers." These are especially useful for living daily in our Baptism and for preparing either for individual confession or especially for the reception of the Sacrament of the Altar (Holy Communion). There are twenty questions, and the first ten are a good summary of the Law that shows our sin and the Gospel that shows our Savior (the second ten prepare the Christian to receive Holy Communion):

1. Do you believe that you are a sinner?
   Yes, I believe it. I am a sinner.

2. How do you know this?
   From the Ten Commandments, which I have not kept.

3. Are you sorry for your sins?
   Yes, I am sorry that I have sinned against God.

4. What have you deserved from God because of your sins?
   His wrath and displeasure, temporal death, and eternal damnation. See Rom. 6:21, 23.

5. Do you hope to be saved?
   Yes, that is my hope.

6. In whom then do you trust?
   In my dear Lord Jesus Christ.

7. Who is Christ?
   The Son of God, true God and man.

8. How many Gods are there?
   Only one, but there are three persons: Father, Son, and Holy Spirit.

9. What has Christ done for you that you trust in Him?
   He died for me and shed His blood for me on the cross for the forgiveness of sins.

10. Did the Father also die for you?
    He did not. The Father is God only, as is the Holy Spirit; but the Son is both true God and true man. He died for me and shed His blood for me.

PERSPECTIVE

This is the top of the engagement triangle. Our perspective is the life-giving Word of God, but we must be aware that the Word of God has two themes, two ways, or two basic messages: the Law and the Gospel. It is essential that we keep them distinct as *they have different purposes.* The Law's main purpose is to show our need to be saved on account of our sin. The Gospel's main purpose is to show our Savior, who came to cover our sin with His precious blood and win for us eternal life. With this perspective of humanity's great malady or need and of God's universal answer, which is faith in Christ, the Savior of the world, we have a grid or an organizing principle for our **perspective** on top of the engagement triangle. This is where we must begin.

The Law May or May Not Be Necessary in Engagement

People in the world today are inundated by sinful influences, and there are many responses to this predicament. One reaction is to embrace it and allow our sin to run amok. After all, everyone else is doing it, and this is "just what happens in life." Surely, no one expects us to enter a monastery! When we play this game of moral compromise, our consciences begin to deteriorate, and before you know it, our hearts become hardened as we begin to justify our sin more and more. It is easy to see that our great nation is reminiscent of the condition that once prevailed in Israel: "Everyone did what was right in his own eyes" (Judges 17:6; 21:25). The practical result in the soul of the person who gets caught up in this is that he or she becomes *comfortable in his or her sin. If a person is in this position, then engagement must at some point offer God's Law that identifies whatever is against God's Law as sin.* This is the primary purpose of the Law: to reveal sin (Romans 3:20). This simple fact suffers the most intense and irate reaction from the world. It is identified as the basis for the greatest evils in the world, and those who hate the faith use this as the reason for accusing Christianity of inciting bigotry and spiritual abuse. To hold belief in such a divine Law is to maintain the position of judge, and this is what is responsible for so much of the hatred in the world. This is how the argument goes, anyway.

This, of course, is a supreme irony. The very thing—the Law—that would help a person see their greatest need is attacked by sin, the world, and the devil as that which should be eliminated. Keep in mind that we are *not* saying that the Law itself saves anyone. It doesn't. We *are* saying, however, that the Law is necessary to awaken a person from their slumber and complacency in the face of sin. Why would anyone ever want to address a problem if they are completely unaware of having one?

This is the reason the Law is necessary. It is, in fact, vital. If not for the Law, we would never know what sin is. St. Paul instructs, "For I would not have known what it is to covet if the law had not said, 'You shall not covet'" (Romans 7:7). In this way—because the Law accuses and uncovers our sin, which would otherwise destroy us—"the law is holy, and the commandment is holy and righteous and good" (Romans 7:12).

Even in the face of the worldly assault and accusation to keep silent about the Law of God, Christians must remain faithful in giving the Law to those for whom Christ died when their conscience has grown dim and sin is approved of and defended. The pressure to keep silent and allow sin to perpetuate is tremendous, but Christians mustn't give in to fear. In the big picture, when the Law is maintained, then people are truly helped and blessed. Then they are put in a position to earnestly seek God's help. That is when people are ready for the Gospel.

This situation, however, does not always apply. There are times when others without the Gospel, while not seeking to justify sin, feel a tremendous burden as Lawbreakers (even if it is only through the natural law of conscience). Such people already know—without anyone telling them—that something is terribly wrong with their lives. These people are *not* comfortable in their sin, but they are rather greatly *burdened* and *alarmed* by their sin. *People in this position do not need the Law during engagement.* The Holy Spirit has already prepared their conscience to receive the Gospel that God in Christ has forgiven their sin and that overflowing and eternal life is theirs. When this happens, people *want* to live for God as a result of having received God's great gift to them in Christ.

When the Law *Is* Necessary, It Sheds Light on Particular Sins, but We Don't Obsess about Them

While the Catechism provides the Christian with a clear Law-Gospel perspective, the next question is, "Okay, how do I share the Law in engagement when a person needs to hear it?" This is an extremely important question, and the answer is vital for successful engagement.

To blurt out accusation with the Law as a way of introduction is a great way to sabotage any hope for engagement. Here, we are blessed by our Lord's example when He spoke to the woman in Samaria (John 4).

There are three major things that happened there that apply to our current consideration:

1. The Lord *engaged the woman* and found a way to keep the engagement flowing (the discussion about water, both natural water and *the* water Christ gives for eternal life).

2. The Lord called out her *sins* (plural) with respect to her sexual immorality (her several husbands and current fornication).

3. The Lord did not, however, obsess about her *sins* (plural), but rather focused on her greater need, namely, her *sin* (singular): *"you worship what you do not know"* (v. 22).

What the Law Should Emphasize

The most important first step in engagement with Law affirms that the sin problem needs to be exposed, but this is precisely why engagement is so important. What people say up front, or what they seem to represent even before they say a word, is often *not* the *issue; it is not the core sin.* I have a lot of children, and over the years when a problem came up, I would ask them, "What's wrong?" I would often get one of two answers: either "I don't know," or an answer that wasn't really the answer because often *they* didn't even know what the problem was. At this point, it is easy to waste a lot of time and energy as we address the answers that are only misdirections. What hardly ever happens is that we get the answers we immediately need to know so that we know what's *really* going on.

Children and teenagers, however, aren't the only ones who do this. The Law properly used gets at the *core of the sin problem.* If we expend our energy talking about the surface stuff, especially if we come off as moralists, legalists, or snobby judges, we will never be given the chance to engage about why all actual sins even exist.

While we must often address actual sins as the first step toward being alarmed by our sin condition, sometimes Christians get carried away feeling good about how well they can criticize actual sins. What some people call "speaking the Law" is just being boldly obnoxious and cruel. This feels good to the sinful nature, coinciding with the temptation in the Garden of Eden to be like God (Genesis 3:5). Sinners like pontificating on what is good and evil. This problem is within every Christian on the planet, and the bad habit turns quickly into what Jesus warned about when He said the rulers of the Gentiles would "lord it over them" (Matthew 20:25). Toss God's Law into the mix, and it's easy for someone to feel as though they are speaking for God.

Let us be clear: it is one thing for the Holy Law—when properly wielded—to, indeed, judge; but it is another thing for a person to get on a power trip while scrutinizing sins. The Law produces a serious diagnosis that causes alarm, while people who like to judge want to shove it in the face of their enemies. There's a big difference. Christians who use Law mourn the sin condition they share with those without Christ, but others use the Law so that they can stroke their egos while pointing their fingers. These do not represent the heart of Christ.

Our goal, however, is to get to the point of the engagement that needs the Law and not overreact to something that makes us uncomfortable or something we disagree with along the way. For example, people often enter objectionable lifestyles, not because they are looking to break a specific commandment, but because they are trying to address a visceral thing in their heart. Why do people do the things they do? Often it is because of anger, shame, guilt, or fear. These basic things are at the root of most anything else they do. But if we magnify the symptomatic sins, we may never get to the heart of the matter. Again, this does not mean that we do not apply the Law to actual sins, but we don't remain stuck there. We don't want to lose the forest (the desperate condition of the heart) for the trees (those symptoms of the greater problem). We just say enough about actual sins to indicate that there is a deeper problem going on. When it becomes evident that the Christian isn't out to win an argument but cares *more* about the person without Christ, then we can focus on the more critical need.

God's Law is not given for us to play around with; it is given to show us that we are *by nature sinful and unclean*. The Law is given to reveal when shame is driving a person to every manifestation of that problem imaginable. It does no good to harp on that person like an irritating moralist, but rather, we need the Law to take us to the heart of the matter.

The Law primarily shows us that there is a problem between us and God. Until this is properly addressed by the Gospel, people will live with big holes in their souls. They will sense that something is wrong with them, even as they desperately try to hide it.

How does this translate in the practical sharing of the Law? It translates when we are confronted with any ethical or moral issue that disagrees with the Christian faith, but we refuse to lambast anyone for any social issue. We can say boldly whether a social issue is against God's Word and will, but if we make this our preoccupation, then any potential engagement will deteriorate into both parties becoming argumentative. We must remember this: *as long as core inherited sin is not addressed, the unbeliever will simply not be convinced that their actual sins are problematic.* So why on earth would we insist on pounding actual sins?!

Jim Peterson helps us sense the good tension we are speaking of here: "The ability to see beyond the surface symptom to the true need is the key to establishing honest relationships with non-Christians. We do not have to condone their behavior to accept and love them."[7]

In other words, the Law is not given primarily for us to nitpick for a pietistic, holier-than-thou, fault-finding mission, but the Law is given, rather, to uncover the enormous hole that people live with that is sin in the most important sense of the word: a spiritual disease that permeates the whole being of a person, a problem so severe that it separates us from God.

Here, we remember that people are not sinful because they commit sins, but rather, they commit sins because they are sinful. C. S. Lewis asserted: "A recovery of the old sense of sin is essential to Christianity."[8] Until this happens, we will be "deceived by looking on the outside of things."[9] In another place, Lewis wrote: "Unchastity, anger, greed,

---

[7]   Jim Petersen, *Living Proof* (Colorado Springs, CO: NavPress, 1989), 58.

[8]   C. S. Lewis, *The Problem of Pain*, Macmillan Paperback Edition (New York: Macmillan, 1962), 57.

[9]   Lewis, *The Problem of Pain*, 59.

drunkenness, and all that, are mere fleabites in comparison: it was through Pride that the devil became the devil: Pride leads to every other vice: it is the complete anti-God state of mind."[10] Phillip Max Johnson sheds light on "sins" and "sin":

> Our *sins* are the concrete expression of our *sin*. Our sins mark us as moral and spiritual failures and wrongdoers; our sin marks us as enemies of God and destined for death. "Sin," as the theologians teach us, is a relational concept: "*Against you only* have I sinned, and done what is evil *in your sight*" [Psalm 51:4]. Whereas, "sins" is a behavioral term.[11]

When a Person Sees Their Need, We Share the Gospel That Gives What *All* People Yearn For: Life

St. Paul wrote that the ministry he conducted was "for the sake of the gospel" (1 Corinthians 9:23). The *Gospel* or the *Good News* is that God, in and through His Son, Jesus Christ, has fulfilled *the greatest longing* of humanity (eternal life) and defeated *the greatest dreading* of humanity (eternal death). This is why St. Paul was so focused on the Gospel. The center of the Gospel is Jesus Christ, so Paul also wrote, "For I decided to know nothing among you except Jesus Christ and Him crucified" (1 Corinthians 2:2). By focusing on Christ, Paul knew that he would always keep God's greatest gift to humanity clearly before him. By virtue of what Jesus has done for everyone, this Good News is "the power of God for salvation to everyone who believes" (Romans 1:16).

It's important to steer away from making this a *religious* thing that somehow strays from *real life*. Much to the contrary, the Gospel addresses the heart of what is important to all people. Simply said, the single greatest instinct, desire, and drive in the hearts of human beings is to *live*. No matter what drives people or what people say to define themselves, people—all people—embrace life. Even people despairing

---

[10] Lewis, *Mere Christianity*, 122.

[11] Phillip Max Johnson, "Exposed by the Light: Confessing Our Sin and Naming Our Sins," *Lutheran Forum* (Fall 1997), 15.

of life—despairing because their *life* has been severely hurt—yearn for a better life. They, too, want to live in fullness and joy. Even a person who says they want to die is really crying out that they desire that their life be unimpaired (be it physically, emotionally, or spiritually).

The bottom line is that we want life while sensing that life can be or ought to be good. We desire life not just for seventy or eighty years, or even 120 years, but life that doesn't stop. The Socratic resignation "death is a part of life" is a rationalization, and deep down, it is entirely unsatisfactory. Once a person tastes the gift of life, they don't want it to end. God knows this. He created us for life, and He desires that we may enjoy it—literally—forever. God has done something about our great yearning: it's encapsulated in the *Gospel*.

The Gospel is the astounding good news that God has given His Son, Jesus Christ, to give us the gift of eternal life through His blood, which, in the eyes of God, covers our sin, which would otherwise keep us from eternal life. Jesus said, "I came that they may have life and have it abundantly" (John 10:10). God through His Son, Jesus—who entered our humanity in time and space—came to address this most vital thing: He came to give life that doesn't end. When physical death comes, all who trust in the One who conquered death for all people experience the victory of Christ's resurrection: first in that they continue to live in spirit in the presence of God (what is known as *heaven*), but then, most importantly, in that they will experience the day when their living spirit will be rejoined to their resurrected and glorified body. What is our assurance of this? It is the historical fact of Christ's resurrection. Christians are Christians because they know that death doesn't have the last word. "And this is the testimony, that God gave us eternal life, and this life is in His Son. Whoever has the Son has life" (1 John 5:11–12).

Jesus: The *Whole-Person* Savior

St. Matthew was a publican, a tax collector. From a societal point of view, it was difficult to be any lower than a tax collector. Tax collectors and prostitutes were the scum of the earth. It is remarkable that when Jesus passed by Matthew, He did not address his greed, deceit, or robbery. Jesus didn't even call him on his blatant idolatry. Instead, we have this recorded in God's Word: "As Jesus passed on from there, He saw a man called Matthew sitting at the tax booth, and He said to him, 'Follow Me.' And he rose and followed Him" (Matthew 9:9). Can you imagine what Jesus *could have said* about Matthew? But He didn't. Matthew was suffering in a life that was separated from God. No other symptomatic sin compared with this deadly virus in his heart. Jesus did not call Matthew to give up some specific vice or sin. Instead, Jesus called Matthew to follow Him. He addressed Matthew's *whole life*. Jesus cares about our being spiritually dead (Ephesians 2:1), not about the fact that our deadness causes a stench. If Jesus was only concerned about the stench (the symptoms), He might have commanded Matthew to clean things up. But instead, Jesus addressed Matthew's need for a new life.

This is the key to understanding the significance of Christ's parable of the Pharisee and tax collector. The Pharisees were known for detail, the counting of laws, and the emphasis on external conduct and superficial law-keeping: all symptomatic things. The tax collector in the parable could not have cared less about these things, though he committed many more outward sins than the Pharisee did. The tax collector's preoccupation was on *his whole person*. The different viewpoints are evident in the parable:

> The Pharisee, standing by himself, prayed thus: "God, I thank You that I am not like other men, extortioners, unjust, adulterers, or even like this tax collector. I fast twice a week; I give tithes of all that I get." But the tax collector, standing far off, would not even lift up his eyes to heaven, but beat his breast, saying, "God, be merciful to me, a sinner." (Luke 18:11–13)

Jesus went on to commend the tax collector, who would be lifted up by God's mercy, but He spoke judgment against the self-righteous Pharisee. How do we know all our sins (plural) are forgiven? We know when our *sinful person* (singular condition) is forgiven. When we know that this is what Jesus does for us, then our shame is overwhelmed by the forgiveness of our whole being, our entire *person*. To truly confess the forgiveness of sin is to confess that by ourselves, our entire life is wrong, but through Christ and His forgiveness, we are now completely right in the eyes of God. Only then do we begin to work on the details according to God's will. Sanctification can only follow justification; it can never precede it. Consider carefully how Jesus conducted Himself around people known for their manifest sins:

> And as Jesus reclined at table in the house, behold, many tax collectors and sinners came and were reclining with Jesus and His disciples. And when the Pharisees saw this, they said to His disciples, "Why does your teacher eat with tax collectors and sinners?" But when [Jesus] heard it, He said, "Those who are well have no need of a physician, but those who are sick. Go and learn what this means, 'I desire mercy, and not sacrifice.' For I came not to call the righteous, but sinners." (Matthew 9:10–13)

Those who are self-deceived in their false sense of righteousness are preoccupied with the details, using the simple—but flawed—logic that to avoid sinful behavior and sinful acts cancels the sin problem. This is a deadly misunderstanding. It's deadly because such an outlook doesn't need Jesus. They don't need a physician. They think they're fine and healthy. But Jesus becomes a great Savior indeed when people do not limit Him to this or that sinful behavior, but when they see that Jesus has come for *the whole sinner*. For these, Jesus has come. This is the Gospel.

CHAPTER 1 DISCUSSION GUIDE

ENGAGEMENT'S PERSPECTIVE (LAW AND GOSPEL)

UNCOVER INFORMATION

1. The top of the engagement triangle is the Word of God. What are the two themes, two ways, or two basic messages of God's Word?

2. When is God's Law necessary? What does the world try to do with it? Why does the world have this reaction toward the Law?

3. When is God's Law *not* needed in engagement?

4. We don't obsess over actual sins, so what should the Law emphasize?

5. What is the Gospel?

Discover Meaning

1. How does Judges 17:6; 21:25 describe our current culture?

2. What is ironic about the world's need for God's Law and the world's reaction toward it?

3. How might a person already know the Law—while not knowing God's Word, per se—before you begin to engage them?

4. How does John 4 about Jesus and the woman from Samaria help us to learn about engagement? Explain what Jesus did in this exchange through the three points listed.

5. Examine the quotes by C. S. Lewis and Phillip Max Johnson about "the old sense of sin," "complete anti-God state of mind," and "our sin marks us as enemies of God." Why is this main problem to be addressed?

Explore Implications

1. Because of the world's reaction against God's Law, why is the Christian tempted to remain silent about the Law?

2. If all actual sins stream from the core sin—the sinful nature, original sin, spiritual disease—then why are we unwise to hammer or obsess over actual sins?

3. What could happen to a person if they never discover their core spiritual disease?

4. Why are the Gospel and the theme of life so closely associated?

5. What does it mean that Jesus came "for the whole sinner"? What does it mean that the Gospel knows no limits in dealing with sin (not counting the rejection of the Gospel itself)?

CHAPTER 2:
ENGAGEMENT'S PEOPLE
(ONE-ON-ONE)

The Catechism Teaches Us about People

The Creed not only teaches about God but also about people, *all* people. These things help us when we arrive at our second point of the engagement triangle: **people**. It is helpful to reflect on what we learn from the meanings of the articles of the Creed that especially pertain to the people we engage with. These are highlights of the anthropological aspects of the Creed:

> **Explanation of the First Article:** I believe that God has made me and all creatures; that He has given me my body and soul, eyes, ears, and all my members, my reason and all my senses, and still takes care of them.

> **Explanation of the Second Article:** [Jesus Christ] has redeemed me, a lost and condemned person, purchased and won me from all sins, from death, and from the power of the devil; not with gold or silver, but with His holy, precious blood and with His innocent suffering and death, that I may be His own and live under Him in His kingdom and serve Him in everlasting righteousness, innocence, and blessedness, just as He is risen from the dead, lives and reigns to all eternity.

Explanation of the Third Article: I believe that I cannot by my own reason or strength believe in Jesus Christ, my Lord, or come to Him; but the Holy Spirit has called me by the Gospel, enlightened me with His gifts, sanctified and kept me in the true faith.

PEOPLE

People Are the Same and Different at the Same Time

God's Word reveals how people are the same: we are all sinners who have strayed from God and need something to be done about that fact. We all know something is awry; something is missing. Because of this one thing, we aren't exactly all that comfortable with having to face death, even if we go on about how we aren't afraid of it. What makes people different, however, is to what extent they will acknowledge their need, their intrinsic awareness of the problem, and how and what they're doing about death being on the horizon. That is, people are the same and different at the same time, but at the end of the day, there is a great equalizer among people: *we all have a head and heart problem.*

The Universal Head and Heart Problem

In considering the head (objective knowing), God's Word says, "The natural person does not accept the things of the Spirit of God, for they are folly to him, and he is not able to understand them because they are spiritually discerned" (1 Corinthians 2:14). As for the heart (subjective experience), God's Word pulls no punches about this stark reality: "The heart is deceitful above all things, and desperately sick; who can understand it?" (Jeremiah 17:9). There are some immediate ramifications that flow from these Scriptures:

1. The natural condition of a person predisposes them to resist accepting the Gospel. In fact, the Scriptures state at 1 Corinthians 1:18: "For the word of the cross is folly to those who are perishing." The Christian should *never* be surprised or put off by a negative response, and it would be silly to take it personally.

2. The Christian will remember that the Holy Spirit is calling the shots. He works when and where He pleases. We are called to be patient. Sometimes, Christians are put to the test: Will we love a person enough not to give up on them? Will we wait for the Holy Spirit to choose the right time?

3. The Christian will therefore be willing to share the Law and Gospel over and over again without becoming obnoxious or rude toward skepticism, knowing that some people just need more time to come to faith.[12] In this way, Christians show great tolerance in the face of intolerance.

Knowing the Severity of People's Spiritual Problem

In his powerful essay "Salvation within Our Reach," Ronald F. Marshall presents a powerful elaboration of the spiritual problem from the Lutheran Confessions and from Luther:

> [Christians] are to teach and believe that sin is so pervasive that it is from "head to Foot" (SA III.3.35); so damaging that it makes us into "recalcitrant donkeys" (SD VI.24), and extreme enough to make us even "hate God" (Ap II.11). It makes us wicked by being *incurvatus in se*—curved in on ourselves (LW 25: 345,513). So the twisted nature reported in Romans 7:23 as "captivity" must not be limited to pre-Christian days but

---

[12] See my account in *Faith That Sees through the Culture* (St. Louis: Concordia Publishing House, 2018) about "Paul," pages 65-68. This former agnostic who came to saving faith had stated his skepticism to me several times. I kept reminding him that God loved him, forgave his sins, and won for him eternal life through Christ over and over again, until he finally held my hand and told me in tears, "I believe!"

extended to all of Christian life (LW 25:331,339 vs. Käsemann [*Commentary on Romans*] 192,200). This teaching on sin will also change the way we think of The Church. No longer will it be seen as a club, school, meeting hall, or community activity center, but as a "hospital" for the spiritually, terminally ill (LW 17:66; *Sermons* 3:26).[13]

The Image of God and Reason

Genesis 1:27 clearly teaches that when God first created man—male and female—He created them "in His own image." God commanded our first parents not to eat from the tree of the knowledge of good and evil (Genesis 2:17). This should not be construed as having been a dangling carrot for temptation. They already had everything they could want that was good. Before their rebellion and fall, they even had full access to the tree of life (Genesis 2:16; 3:22). The tree of the knowledge of good and evil was rather like a visible sign of God's Word. It called out, "Trust God," and as they did, they remained fantastically blessed. To turn away from God and His Word, however, results in death. Indeed, this was exactly what God had warned the man about regarding the tree of the knowledge of good and evil (Genesis 2:17).

The rebellion occurred when the man and woman disobeyed God (Genesis 3:6). And the Church has taught for two millennia that God stayed true to His warning: death came. With death having entered man, man lost the image of God. But what was the image of God? It was "original righteousness," meaning man shared in God's righteousness. Man shared God's goodness and holiness so that God's thoughts were man's thoughts and God's ways man's ways.[14] It also meant that "the reason of man would be surrendered to God; his will to his reason; his feeling and all other faculties to his will. Hence all the powers and faculties in man would constitute a perfect harmony."[15] But with the

---

[13] Ronald F. Marshall, "Salvation within Our Reach," *Lutheran Forum* (Fall 1997): 18.

[14] The fall of man caused the exact opposite condition: "For My thoughts are not your thoughts, neither are your ways My ways, declares the Lord" (Isaiah 55:8).

[15] Martin Chemnitz and Johann Gerhard, *The Doctrine of Man in Classical Lutheran Theology*, ed. Herman A. Preus and Edmund Smits, trans. Mario Colacci et al. (Minneapolis: Augsburg, 1962), 38.

loss of the image of God, the condition of original righteousness and its bearing on man's reason to surrender to God was also lost.

At the same time, "It is not that will, feelings, and faculties are lost, but that they are now utterly out of sorts, no longer working in harmony. That is, the *imago Dei* is not a substance or exceptional trait, it is not a faculty, and it is not to be confused with the soul or the parts of man himself."[16] With these details in mind, we can now deal with what some people say is a contradiction: "How can you say that the image of God was lost when *after* the fall, Genesis 9:6 and James 3:9 refer to people as still being in the image of God?" The answer is that there is both a *narrow* sense of the image of God and a *broad* sense of the image of God. Yes, man lost original righteousness (narrow sense of the image of God), but there is still a broad sense of the image of God that remains even in the unregenerate. Johann Gerhard, considered one of the three greatest classical Lutheran theologians (only Luther and Chemnitz are above him), provides further clarity:

> If the image of God refers to some moral principles which are born in us and with us and which consist in some tiny remnants of the divine image in the mind and will of man, then too with regard to these most minute particles we maintain that the image of God was not utterly lost. In fact, the work of the Law is still written in the hearts of men [Romans 2:15], even of the unregenerate.[17]

There is without a doubt a radical difference between man's reason before and after the fall.

Luther warned against fallen reason: "Reason is the devil's prostitute and can do nothing but blaspheme and defile everything God speaks and does."[18] Luther was writing about reason *after* the fall, and this is

---

Page references to Concordia Publishing House reprint in 1982.

[16] Alfonso Odilon Espinosa, "Apologetics in Pastoral Theology," in *Theologia et Apologia: Essays in Reformation Theology and Its Defense Presented to Rod Rosenbladt*, ed. Adam S. Francisco, Korey D. Maas, and Steven P. Mueller (Eugene, OR: Wipf & Stock, 2007), 325.

[17] Chemnitz and Gerhard, *Doctrine of Man*, 62.

[18] Martin Luther, *What Luther Says: A Practical In-Home Anthology for the Active Christian*, comp.,

why Luther wrote in the Small Catechism that there is no coming to God by one's own reason. *This state of affairs, however, does not mean that there is no point of contact between the Christian and unbeliever.* While an entire chapter is coming up on "Engagement's Example" (chapter 6) that will focus on Acts 17, there is something from this text pertinent to the current consideration:

> Perhaps the classic scriptural example of [this point of contact] is St. Paul at the Areopagus in Acts 17. St. Paul's use of reason and rationality is painstakingly lucid. It is exciting to see St. Paul appealing to the Athenians' natural knowledge of God. Though their knowledge is darkened and pluralistic, St. Paul builds upon it by presenting the doctrine of creation and the creator. He goes on to apply the work of the law by correcting the limitations placed on God via temples made by man and images formed by the art and imagination of man, and reasonably shows the superiority of the one raised from the dead.[19]

What is described here is what I like to refer to as "the hook of engagement."[20] Alister McGrath gives an insightful elaboration on what is already taught about the natural knowledge of God in Romans 1 (observation of creation) and Romans 2 (awareness of conscience): "Reason, then, provides an important point of contact for the gospel. Though fallen, reason still possesses the ability to grasp and point, however darkly, toward the reality of God."[21] Engagement seeks *the hook* as St. Paul did with the Athenians so that he could then proceed with the only thing that turns people to God: the Gospel of the resurrected Christ.

Ewald M. Plass (St. Louis: Concordia Publishing House, 1959), 1161.

[19] Espinosa, "Apologetics in Pastoral Theology," 322.

[20] I first used this terminology in *Theologia et Apologia,* page 323, but I use it in a more expansive way here as I am not limiting the idea to apologetics.

[21] Alister E. McGrath, *Intellectuals Don't Need God & Other Modern Myths: Building Bridges to Faith through Apologetics* (Grand Rapids, MI: Zondervan, 1993), 37.

Engagement Is Intentional and Noninvasive

Rev. Mark Jasa has met astounding success engaging those without faith in Christ by being both intentional (looking for opportunities to engage) and noninvasive. This approach to engagement puts the Christian in the best position to connect with people.[22] But do your eyes deceive you? Did you just read the word *intentional*?! *Intentional engagement* is assuredly the single most terrifying potential activity on the face of the planet! Isn't it well known that if any Christian does this, they might melt or spontaneously combust? By recommending *intentional engagement,* have we just effectively eliminated all introverted, shy, tired, bashful, busy, inconsiderate, and, oh yeah, still confessing-their-sin Christians from the possibility of engagement? Pastor Jasa warns, however, that if we insist that engagement will *not* occur *until* the unbeliever makes the first move or asks us about the faith, then we might be waiting for the rest of our lives (we will put the word *asks* in 1 Peter 3:15 in perspective later). But how can we be intentional—and feel good about it—without feeling like we're trying to sell something, pressure someone, or acting like a religious fanatic?

The key here is that Christians are not *trying to foist their agenda, but rather, they are trying to love people: notice, greet, smile, be kind, and be ready to help!* Who knows, you might find yourself talking to someone face-to-face (and live)! Don't worry! God has given His baptized people His Spirit. He intends to work through those in Christ, through their holding to His Word and by emulating His love. "We love because He first loved us" (1 John 4:19).

Still, some Christians will start to sweat at the prospect of intentional engagement. Let's try to nip this in the bud: my wife, Traci, and I have been blessed over the years to serve children in various capacities (e.g., foster care). Once, we were matched with children who came from a very isolated part of the state and for various reasons were hardly ever taken out. They had, for example, never been to a shopping mall. Traci and I thought it would be fun to open their eyes to some new experiences.

---

22   Jasa, interview.

Nothing could have prepared me for what I witnessed in the mall. The children were utterly taken aback—eyes fully dilated, fight-or-flight instincts initiated—by this tall, steel contraption that was, for lack of a better description, a moving staircase. I could tell that this thing was causing all kinds of cognitive dissonance in them. After all, the steps on this thing were being swallowed up top, and when they came back down on the other side, the steps disappeared into the floor. At first, the kids were freaked out, and trust me, their first instinct was *not to get on!* Who could blame them? They had never done it before. Suffice it to say, however, that over time that day, they did not want to stop getting on and off! How did they go from near terror to delighted confidence? *They stepped out.*

I don't see Pastor Jasa foaming at the mouth, chanting a mantra to himself "share the faith, share the faith, share the faith." Rather, *I see Pastor Jasa stepping out to be friendly,* to acknowledge people, to ask how they are doing. And then, if the Lord permits a conversation to ensue, *he is simply willing to share the wonderful news that God loves them and that it's true because God's Son, Jesus Christ, died to forgive all their sins!* Pastor Jasa also relieves those he teaches in terms of the memorization of Scripture. Though memorizing Scripture is a great thing, too many Christians psych themselves out thinking that they must be able to quote Scripture left and right. Not at all. Pastor Jasa recommends we memorize one verse in particular—a short but powerful one: "Behold, the Lamb of God, who takes away the sin of the world" (John 1:29).

Engagement for the Gospel That Is Both Good and True

John 1:29 is good news! God through Jesus *takes away sin.* Therefore, we don't have to live in shame or fear or dread. God—who created the heavens and the earth—is *for us!* One day, a young atheist told Pastor Jasa that she was afraid of death. Pastor Jasa told her, "Don't worry about death. Jesus is your Savior!" To which she replied, "That would be good news if it were true." Pastor Jasa, therefore, encourages to share the Gospel as being *both* good *and* true.[23]

---

[23] Jasa, interview.

The Gospel may sound very good indeed, but if it isn't true, then, to put it mildly, Christianity has a big problem. If something is good but not true, what good is it? If something is true but not good, then thanks, but no thanks! But if something is *both* good *and* true, now we have something compelling.

Pastor Jasa shared his strategy with me as he presents what is true: *he strives not to argue, but to agree.* He does this so he can demonstrate that the Gospel resonates with what people know to be true. This doesn't mean he compromises the Gospel in any way, but he has learned that when people state objections to the truth of the Gospel, he listens carefully and then asks about their *reasons* for their objections, all the while treating them with gentleness and respect.

People will—if you ask them gently and respectfully—often divulge their underlying reasons for questioning the truth of the Gospel. Then, with this information, Pastor Jasa will ask the person *to apply their reason* (their litmus or standard) *to other things in life*, be it upon other religious systems, historical knowledge, or the way they function day to day. By doing this, he is agreeing with whatever he *can* agree with in terms of the legitimacy of various standards of history, logic, morality, and so on.

For example, if a person questions the historicity of the Gospel, then we ask about their standards for trusting recorded history. With their standard revealed, we might ask them if their standard applies to something like Alexander the Great conquering the Persians in 333 BC or Julius Caesar crossing the Rubicon in 49 BC. If they do this, then Pastor Jasa *will apply their own standard to the resurrection of the Lord Jesus Christ.*

Or let's say they insist that another world religion or spiritual perspective is more appealing to them. Pastor Jasa will not start to argue against that position. Instead, he will ask what it is they hope to get from that faith system. If they share this information, then Pastor Jasa will ask them *whether they are keeping its standards, because all other systems are law or performance-based.* The moment the person admits to uncertainty (if they're being honest), Pastor Jasa demonstrates how the

Gospel isn't like that. In doing this, Pastor Jasa *affirms their standard, but then demonstrates a real answer to their dilemma in the Gospel.*

His goal is to "turn it around and talk about the facts," as he puts it, and then come back to the Gospel to demonstrate its veracity in the face of such standards and longings. In every case, he returns to the Gospel as *both* good *and* true.

The Christian faith's alignment with real history, early manuscripts, and eyewitnesses who gave their lives for the Gospel—if nothing else—demonstrates that it is an *intelligent* faith. "Christianity is in no sense irrational; indeed, its own system of rationality is perfectly coherent."[24] The Christian faith serves intellects that need truth and human experience that values what is good. Pastor Jasa says we serve both through the Gospel that proclaims what is good (God's forgiveness of sins and gift of eternal life in Christ) and what is true (through the veracity of a historically verifiable faith).[25]

---

[24] Alister E. McGrath, *A Fine-Tuned Universe: The Quest for God in Science and Theology*, Gifford Lectures, 2009 (Louisville, KY: Westminster John Knox Press, 2009), 37.

[25] Rev. Jasa teaches that we must consider both the intelligence and the experience of people.

CHAPTER 2 DISCUSSION GUIDE

ENGAGEMENT'S PEOPLE (ONE-ON-ONE)

UNCOVER INFORMATION

1. How are people the same and different at the same time?

2. What is the natural predisposition of people toward the Gospel?

3. Who is "calling the shots" in engagement for sharing Christ?

4. What was the original "image of God"? When this was lost, what resulted in people?

5. At the very end of the chapter, Pastor Jasa teaches that when we engage we should take two things into consideration about people. What are they?

DISCOVER MEANING

1. What are the "head" problem and the "heart" problem of all people (according to the sinful nature)?

2. Our core sin problem is referred to as *incurvatus in se.* How does this translate, and how does this help us understand the basic tendency of the sinful nature?

3. With respect to the discussion on the image of God, what is the "hook of engagement"?

4. In what sense do Genesis 9:6 and James 3:9 teach that people still have an "image of God," but no longer in the sense prior to the fall of man in Genesis 3?

5. How can engagement be both intentional *and* noninvasive?

EXPLORE IMPLICATIONS

1. What are the three implications affecting engagement that pertain to "the head and the heart"?

2. If there is still a "broad sense" of the image of God, what is the implication of this insofar as it pertains to engagement?

3. What's wrong with objectivizing unbelievers as "potential notches" on the Christian's evangelistic belt?

4. Why is it so important to present the Gospel as *both* good *and* true?

5. These two things in the question above touch on the fact that people are both *intellectual* and *experiential*. Why is this relevant to us as we engage in order to share Christ?

CHAPTER 3:
ENGAGEMENT'S PLACE
(CULTURE)

The Catechism Teaches Us about Place

It is exciting to see how applicable Luther's Small Catechism is to our consideration of engagement. True to form, Luther has keen insights that touch the third point of the engagement triangle: **place**. The **perspective** (first point) of Scripture informs our **approach** toward engagement; the **people** (second point) remind us of the **attitude** we need for engagement. And now we are in the position to consider how the **culture** (**place**) impacts engagement. But does the Catechism really discuss *culture*? Let me explain a twist here that makes the Christian version of *place* more thorough than what is typically meant by *culture*. And while we will consider the concept more below, allow me to discuss the something *more* that is included in the Christian's place. Place and culture are not entirely the same thing. **Place** includes more than the culture and gives us a fuller description of where we *are*.

PLACE

Wherever the Christian goes, their place includes both a visible and invisible duality.[26] The Christian enters all places with awareness that their interactions with people are affected not only by visible things but also by *invisible* things. Luther's Small Catechism is entirely directed at this reality. Let us consider how the explanation of the Lord's Prayer teaches us about how the Christian should be aware of their environment around them—their *place*—even while in the culture.

These are the two petitions that teach us more about **place**:

The Sixth Petition: And lead us not into temptation.

The Seventh Petition: But deliver us from evil.

Luther is clear on the dangers that are present in our places. We are duly warned, and God prepares us for what places will throw at us:

The Sixth Petition: And lead us not into temptation.

What does this mean? God tempts no one. We pray in this petition that God would guard and keep us so that the devil, the world, and our sinful nature may not deceive us or mislead us into false belief, despair, and other great shame and vice. Although we are attacked by these things, we pray that we may finally overcome them and win the victory.

The Seventh Petition: But deliver us from evil.

What does this mean? We pray in this petition, in summary, that our Father in heaven would rescue us from every evil of body and soul, possessions and reputation, and finally, when our last hour comes, give us a blessed end, and graciously take us from this valley of sorrow to Himself in heaven.

Here is the summary for all our places: put on your seatbelts, because wherever the Christian goes to engage with those without Christ, there

---

[26] Espinosa, *Faith That Sees through the Culture*, chapter 6: "The Lutheran Lens—What Is Real?"

will be forces working to discourage and dissuade engagement for the Gospel. Satan, the world, and sin will seek to envelop and attack with evil all efforts to share Jesus Christ. This sounds scary! But don't lose sight of the great petitions for God to "guard and keep us . . . overcome them and win the victory . . . rescue us from every evil." In Christ, He has, He does, and He will.

The Christian in Culture

Having taken inventory of the invisible realm that contributes to our definition of our places, it's time to include what is usually included in the term *culture*. This, too, is part and parcel of the third point of the engagement triangle. *To ignore the third point is to risk being unaware of external forces that seek to undermine engagement for Christ.* As for **culture**, Martin E. Marty provides a practical definition: "culture is the sum total of the processes and products by which humans do anything and everything to nature (divine creation)."[27]

Marty's definition is helpful because when "humans do anything and everything to nature (divine creation)," the *doing* might be attributed to that which is motivated by faith active in love, sinful impulse, civic duty, and so on. The point is that the end product—culture—is impacted by *a combination of motivations among the people driving "the processes and products by which humans do" what they do within God's creation.*

In the culture, therefore, there are certainly good works of mercy that help people. These might be *both* a civil good work (say through a civic or charitable organization) *and* a good work of living faith in Christ that serves the neighbor in genuine love. What kinds of things in culture are we talking about? Just consider: Hospitals save lives, restaurants feed people, languages facilitate communication, sports provide entertainment, music soothes, art inspires, housing provides shelter, city infrastructure brings order to communities, and even local congregations use cultural resources to facilitate the administration of

---

[27] Martin E. Marty, "Articles of War, Articles of Peace: Christianity and Culture," in *Christ and Culture in Dialogue: Constructive Themes and Practical Applications*, ed. Angus J. L. Menuge (St. Louis: Concordia Academic Press, 1999), 57.

Word and Sacrament (like church furnishings, music, sacred vessels, church architecture, ecclesiastical symbols, etc.). All these things are cultural resources, and we are very much blessed as we employ them.

Having acknowledged the good that can occur within culture, we should not forget the negative influence of the world fueling harmful and destructive actions and behaviors upon the culture. The apostle John warns Christians that they are susceptible to an evil influence:

> Do not love the world or the things in the world. If anyone loves the world, the love of the Father is not in him. For all that is in the world—the desires of the flesh and the desires of the eyes and pride of life—is not from the Father but is from the world. (1 John 2:15–16)

The culture is *affected* by evil in the world when the word *world* itself is representative of a cosmic power driving people to live in sin. On account of this exposure to evil, culture is also the setting for much that is against God. These things also negatively distract and try to stop our best efforts to engage for the sake of the Gospel.

To be sure, this means the Christian struggles both from within (by virtue of the sinful nature) *and* from without (by virtue of the world and Satan) so that while living in the culture, the Christian may be tempted to grow weary of doing good.[28] On account of this, Christians are sinners who often *avoid* Gospel engagement! In the Lord's infinite mercy and wisdom, however, He has provided His Word and Sacraments to keep His people connected to Christ, who has overcome the world (John 16:33).

Culture: Conduit for Engagement

To live in faith holding to King Jesus means that we are in the One who has all power in heaven and on earth (Matthew 28:18). With His love, fear is conquered: "There is no fear in love, but perfect love casts out fear" (1 John 4:18). Why shouldn't fear be cast out? If even the winds

---

[28] Thus St. Paul admonishes, "And let us not grow weary of doing good, for in due season we will reap, if we do not give up" (Galatians 6:9).

and sea obey Him (Matthew 8:27), demons obey Him (Matthew 8:32), health is restored at His word (Matthew 9:6), and death is overcome by Him (Luke 7:14–15; 8:54–55; John 11:43–44), why fear? Jesus said, "Fear not, little flock, for it is your Father's good pleasure to give you the kingdom" (Luke 12:32).

God wants us to know that even though there is much in the culture that will attack faith, it can't beat us. "For everyone who has been born of God overcomes the world. And this is the victory that has overcome the world—our faith. Who is it that overcomes the world except the one who believes that Jesus is the Son of God?" (1 John 5:4–5). St. Paul put it even more simply: "If God is for us, who can be against us?" (Romans 8:31).

At the same time, the Lord *permits* us to live in the culture that threatens our faith. We must trust that God knows exactly what He is doing in and through His engaging people. In fact, He has strategically positioned each of us in the culture. While describing the relationship between Christian apologetics and culture, everything Alister McGrath states here is also applicable to any Christian engaging for the Gospel:

> Christian apologetics is grounded in the knowledge of its audience. This audience is not static and predictable. It is not the same irrespective of its age, social location, country of origin, or language. Rather, it is dynamic and changing. The apologist needs to know his or her audience, speak its language, and share its common flow of life. The best apologists are always found within a society. Those who live in a society know its hopes and its fears. They share its outlook and its images. And they can sense, almost intuitively, the points of contact that exist for the gospel.[29]

Since the Christian lives in the culture, which produces conflict between faith and worldly influences, God permits the Christian to relate to many people who live without Christ in that same culture.

---

[29]   McGrath, *Intellectuals Don't Need God*, 29.

If Christians are *not* in the culture, who will be God's representatives there? In other words, as God allows Christians to experience conflict with culture, *the Christian learns of the very conflicts that block the Gospel for those who are living in the culture without knowledge of the Savior!*

It is a privilege to live in the culture and use what we learn from it to better engage people for the Gospel. What a mission the Lord has given us! In this light, what of the conflict? We are far more blessed that the Lord chose His Church—all the members of the Body of Christ—to engage people in the world at such a time as this, a time when the Gospel is needed most. When hardships are met, we may be encouraged by those who came before us: "Therefore, since we are surrounded by so great a cloud of witnesses, let us also lay aside every weight, and sin which clings so closely, and let us run with endurance the race that is set before us, looking to Jesus, the founder and perfecter of our faith" (Hebrews 12:1–2).

This singular fact about engagement in the culture cannot be over-emphasized: When we get to suffer in the culture, the Lord is at the same time connecting us to those without Christ in the same culture. When culture is shared, we have a God-given segue for engagement. In parts 3 and 4 of this volume, we will consider the special areas in our culture that need the engagement triangle carefully applied. But for now, let's take a moment to see our natural connections, our common *place* with people precisely because we live in the same culture:

Engaging Science: The Christian also shares in the benefits of science.

Engaging Politics: The Christian shares basic political goals like protection and peace.

Engaging Personhood: The Christian has also violated the Fifth Commandment.

Engaging Sexuality: The Christian has also violated the Sixth Commandment.

Engaging Addiction: The Christian is not immune.

> Engaging Depression: The Christian is not incapable of having
> mental illnesses.

In other words, the Christian has *common ground* with people in the culture *at every turn*, because we live in the same culture and are subjected to the same bombardments against the body and soul. God has provided bridges in and through culture for engagement to happen. In spite of all the challenges it brings, this third point in the engagement triangle is not a curse, no matter how lousy it can feel. Culture connects us to engage for Christ.

Only in Our Culture Today

My parishioner came to me with an unusual request: "Pastor, I have a friend whose son, Austin, needs help really bad." There was, however, a catch. I couldn't see him. He was too far away, and besides, Austin had made it known that he didn't want any face-to-face visitors. He was so self-conscious about his appearance and pain that having visitors had become a source of terrible anxiety for him. He was suffering in isolation, and it came out that he was terrified of dying. There were so many unanswered questions, and he felt a million miles away from God. He was a young man with advanced AIDS.

I learned that because he was so emotional over his condition, his best medium for communication was to use a keyboard and just pour his heart out through his fingers. So I offered to "meet" with him computer-to-computer. And that's what we did. We went back and forth many, many times, and up to that point many years ago, I had never become so close to another person while never hearing their voice nor seeing their face. Under such circumstances, the imagination becomes active. What did he look like? Sometimes I just wanted to look into his eyes, and over time, I wished I could just give him a warm embrace.

He was very relieved that a pastor was willing to engage him. When we "met," as we typed long messages to each other, he shared with me that he was full of shame for the way he had lived. He believed that God existed, had a tremendous sense of moral obligation, and did not question the existence of good and evil. Austin also believed that heaven and hell were real. He knew so much already about basic biblical truths, but it became evident that Austin had never known the Gospel.

All his young life, he had operated under the assumption that God was primarily a judge. He expressed that he felt, "Damned if I do, and damned if I don't." If he pursued his sexual desires for other men (which he had), then he felt intrinsic rebellion against God. But if he had tried to hide his desire, he felt that he would have lived with great loneliness. Well, he was lonely now. He felt that no one was going to really hear him bare his soul, much less provide any hope.

The culture's imprints were clearly visible; I was serving someone who had lived in a way the culture had completely affirmed. Yet as he was getting close to dying, Austin felt abandoned by everyone who had once supported his coming out. In addition, this virus was another sign of the times in our culture. The way stage 3 AIDS manifests itself robs a person of all dignity, and to live in a culture *that puts so much stock in appearances*, the despair is palpable. However, the culture had also afforded the use of technology that opened up a way for me to become close to Austin without ever meeting him face-to-face.

Since Austin felt so safe in composing his thoughts on his computer, he bared his soul in a way I had never seen before. He had full license to express himself. He had nothing to lose, and now he was motivated because he believed me when I told him that this was why God had brought us together and I was God's servant, which meant that I was there to serve him. The underlying theme, however, was a universal one: he wanted to love and be loved. It was that simple. Not only had these desires been frustrated through broken relationships, but now he was feeling that because of the way he had lived not even God could love him.

Gently yet boldly, I had the great honor and privilege to share the Gospel with Austin. Jesus had come to rip away from Austin anything and everything he had ever done that offended God by violating His Law—to the extent that Jesus took the blame *for Austin*. And after taking Austin's sin, Christ gave Austin something in return: His purity, righteousness, and holiness. That is how God saw him now!

This transaction is called the *joyous exchange*, and the Gospel is precisely this: *Jesus got your sin, and you got His perfect righteousness!* Now the heavenly Father sees His Son as the sin-bearer and sees you as the one who is clean and holy. God in Christ now counts you as more than acceptable to be in His presence. In fact, there is joy in heaven over you (see Luke 15:7), and God is pleased with you and wants you in His heaven!

The good news, however, didn't stop there for Austin. This Gospel was already true. It wasn't a potentiality. It had already been done! What is more, this Gospel is so powerful, that the Holy Spirit Himself creates the faith to cling to it. Austin told me that for the first time in his life, he knew *why* he could know His Creator was on his side: *on account of Jesus.* Before Austin had come to faith, the cross of Christ was a symbol he never really understood. Why did Jesus hang on the cross? But now, Austin knew. On that cross, Jesus had taken on his sins, and on that cross, Christ had volunteered to claim Austin's curse and shame. He learned that this was the Gospel of the Holy Church for two millennia. This was the Gospel that the martyrs had shed their blood for. This was the Gospel that was and is the power of God for salvation in the lives of real people like Austin (see Romans 1:16).

Over the time we wrote to each other, he grew weaker in his body, but after this young man had received the Gospel, it also seemed that he was getting stronger in his spirit. Despair had been replaced with hope, and this hope was certain and true. But of all the things Austin began to celebrate with me, I think the one thing he celebrated most was that his body, now ravaged with AIDS, was going to rise, be healed and glorified. The day was coming when his scars would be gone, when he would be surging with strength, and when the conflict he had known for so long would be gone, and in its place would be perfect joy and peace. How could he know this? For one reason: Christ had risen from the grave, the powerful result of His royal blood covering sin. In that death, God's blood had made us all holy and full of life, even eternal life. Austin became more than my friend; he became my brother in Christ. I didn't have to see him. I knew him, I loved him, and I get the sneaking suspicion that I will instantly recognize him in heaven someday.

Knowing What to Expect from the Culture and How to Engage It

Since the fall, sin has always been in the world, but it has become increasingly diverse in its manifestations. Having said that, there are some basic cultural values that perpetuate an anti-Christ view. First up is *radical individualism*. In its radical form, it makes people hunger, especially with the constant desire for pleasure and power. This, of course, is nothing new. It is the reverberation of the first sin that gave in to Satan's temptation, "you will be like God" (Genesis 3:5). This, by the way, is not synonymous with the pursuit of happiness as an inalienable right. The Declaration of Independence contextualized this pursuit inherently for the family, the church, and the government. It was, in other words, happiness in community, dependent upon relationships with others. Today's individualism is not that. The current individualism is the antithesis of community.

Alarmingly, this is the opposite view of God's Word: people were simply not created for self-centeredness. God gave us life to have relationship with Him to receive His gifts (and this inherently does not and cannot promote individualism as His gifts are received in His Church that prays "our Father," *not* "my Father"), and God has called us to share His gifts and to love those around us. The new life is led by the Spirit *to get out of self*!

Radical individualism is the foretaste of hell. Hell separates us from real relationship, which begins with God. It is the ultimate state of being alone. Too many people in our culture today are suffering from loneliness, which begins with the mistaken presupposition that life is about living for self. Individualism destroys our ability to be comforted by others, and it loses sight of the skills, talents, and gifts that were given to us by God in order to be a blessing to others.

Individualism's corollary is to live for pleasure. This, too, contradicts the life God has intended for us. Love cannot move inward. Love by its inherent direction is *outward*. It must go out to another person, and as it does, service becomes even more vital than pleasure. Individualism serves self, but love serves the neighbor. The culture can't relate to this. We should not be surprised. Christ said that this was going to become a major problem: "because lawlessness will be increased, the love of many will grow cold" (Matthew 24:12).

Individualism's lustful pursuit for self-pleasure, however, is sinfully justified and maintained through another sign of the culture: *relativism*. Relativism allows the individual the rationale for maintaining self-absorption since truth is determined by self, the individual. Individualism and relativism are convenient bedfellows and combine for a formidable one-two punch toward the formation of a secular worldview devoid of God.

In our culture today, one can still identify considerable diversity, but there seems to be one universal norm and assumption: *truth is relative*. That is, what is *true* is determined by subjective and shifting *taste*. Whether the subjective and shifting taste is popular is beside the point. What *is* universally accepted in relativism is that all ideas are created equal and in themselves are as *true* as any other.

This standard, of course, is not only contrary to the Christian faith, but also to intelligence. Truth is an objective standard that most thinking people would defend, either by its correspondence to an actual state of affairs or by its coherence to logic and reason. If I state that the moon is made of cheese with great conviction and ardent belief, my assertion would simply be false, as rocks are not usually confused with dairy products. Nevertheless, many people behave as if relativism is the chief cornerstone of contemporary culture, no matter how bizarre its assertions may be.

Just one more on this top-three list: after (1) *individualism* is maintained by (2) *relativism*, the culture then has every reason to embrace (3) *skepticism*, which pushes back against any kind of universal truth claim. This will be further discussed in coming chapters, but for now suffice it to say that if Satan can eliminate God's Word through the denial of any objective truth, then the Gospel will never get off the ground. This triad is insidious, and its end result can be catastrophic for the soul.

Thanks be to God, however, that the Christian Church knows what it's up against with regard to the culture: a place inundated with the demonic. At the end of the day, however, all people want to be loved, and this demands we break out of ourselves (we turn away from individualism). All people want a higher authority because they know they aren't God, so we offer Christ, the Truth (we reject relativism). And finally, people want to know that they *can* know (we put away skepticism). People desire and need truth—something reliable, something dependable. All these Jesus gives, and when we're aware of these basic needs, it makes for faith that engages the culture.

CHAPTER 3 DISCUSSION GUIDE

ENGAGEMENT'S PLACE (CULTURE)

UNCOVER INFORMATION

1. What duality of **place** is always surrounding the Christian?

2. Which Chief Part of Luther's Small Catechism informs us about place?

3. What is culture?

4. What kinds of "processes and products" do *you* do and bring to culture?

5. How is there "common ground" for engagement with respect to culture?

DISCOVER MEANING

1. In the explanation of the Sixth Petition, we ask God to guard us from whom specifically?

2. What do the Sixth and Seventh Petitions of the Lord's Prayer teach us about place?

3. Describe culture in a positive sense and then in a negative sense.

4. In what way does 1 John 2:15–16 warn us about the world?

5. Culture is full of individualism, relativism, and skepticism. What do these mean?

EXPLORE IMPLICATIONS

1. If our place includes the invisible, how might this impact our engagement with people?

2. Since the Sixth and Seventh Petitions *do* teach us about place, what should we expect whenever we engage?

3. If someone contributes to a process and product with a self-centered motivation, can God still use that contribution for good? Why or why not?

4. How can culture be such an effective conduit for Gospel engagement when there is so much bad stuff in the culture?

5. Given the three cultural enemies of the faith (individualism, relativism, and skepticism), how does the Gospel offer something better in response to each of these?

PART II:

ENGAGEMENT

TRIANGLE

DEMONSTRATED

CHAPTER 4:
ENGAGEMENT'S APPROACH
(1 PETER 3:15)

Every Christian Called to Be Ready to Testify

The engagement triangle informs us on how to approach anyone to whom we might share Christ: consider **perspective**, **people**, and **place**. Our goal now is to reinforce these three in order again, but this time with Scripture that especially elaborates on each point of the triangle. The first one up is **perspective**, which hones our *approach*, and if there is any Scripture that teaches about engagement's approach, then 1 Peter 3:15 is it. For the sake of some important context to this famous verse, we will begin at verse 14:

> But even if you should suffer for righteousness' sake, you will be blessed. Have no fear of them, nor be troubled, but in your hearts honor Christ the Lord as holy, always being prepared to make a defense to anyone who asks you for a reason for the hope that is in you; yet do it with gentleness and respect.

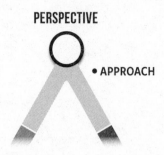

Not only does this Scripture speak to the first point of the engagement triangle, but its context is perfect for the current cultural milieu. Ours is an environment that is not merely post-Christian, but increasingly anti-Christian. St. Peter wrote his first epistle to Christians in "new Gentile congregations . . . enduring significant suffering due to persecution and alienation from the corrupt culture in which they lived" (*TLSB*, p. 2146). That is, we can relate, and St. Peter's letter comes to us at a perfect time.

It's important, however, to back up and take special note of something: 1 Peter 3:15 is absolutely, beyond a shadow of a doubt, presenting a biblical call to all Christians to be ready to speak their faith to those without the Gospel in the culture. In other words, the real transmission of the saving Gospel is *not* reserved for clergy. Pastors and ministers in auxiliary offices are not the only ones who speak and share the Gospel.

The text of 1 Peter 3:15 lucidly presents instruction to everyone who confesses Christ to be ready to give a well-reasoned answer (*defense*, as in a rational testimony to truth) of the Gospel to anyone who asks why the Christian retains hope, especially while they suffer and would otherwise have reason to be afraid. Pastors serving in the office of the ministry preach the Gospel, while Christians who are equipped by the preaching of the Gospel are ready to share the Gospel they've received in their everyday vocations. Luther says, "Here we shall have to admit that St. Peter is addressing these words to all Christians, to priests, laymen, men and women, young and old, and whatever station they are."[30] This is God's plan for the dissemination of the Gospel.

---

[30] AE 30:105.

When the Approach for Engagement Begins

The words of 1 Peter 3:15 are tremendously comforting Scripture for the Christian who desires help when it comes to engaging for Christ and those who don't know His Gospel. Over the years, I have relished being able to encourage Christians who might say, "But I don't know *how* to share the faith!" Without missing a beat, I encourage such Christians by taking them to 1 Peter 3:15 and pointing out *the very first step* for engagement, and it is something *any* Christian can do anytime and anywhere.

It is 100 percent *guaranteed* that a Christian can do this without feeling *any* pressure or anxiety, and on top of that, it is a crucial and non-negotiable first step. There is something else though: when a Christian by the grace of God takes this first step, the Holy Spirit through the Word of Christ will help smooth the path for the rest of engagement. The first step that anyone can do literally makes engagement a realistic expression of faith in the life of the Christian.

What is this first step? The Holy Spirit inspired Peter to write, "But in your hearts honor Christ the Lord as holy." That's it. It is obvious why this first step can be done without pressure or anxiety: the first step is between the Christian and God. The fact is that engagement begins with the Christian's own faith (see *TLSB*, p. 2155). It is an act of faith that should occur *especially* when the Christian suffers for following Christ and might be tempted to fear. The Christian says, "No, even when I suffer, I will not fear, but instead I will set apart Christ the Lord as holy in my heart!"

Engagement begins with confessing Christ as holy and then springing from justifying faith in Christ, living for Christ in holiness. That is, this is not simply a mental affirmation that Christ is holy, but faith that leads to the spiritual fruit of honoring Christ with a holy life.

We cannot begin to say how important this is. What happens when a person is under pressure and suffers? You see the real person come out. When life is easy, the person puts on a good show for others, appearing confident and staying calm. But when life is hard, there is no will for pretending. One is left with the real person. Yes, that real person is also a sinner who suffers under their cross, but they are not only a sinner when they are also in Christ.

Again, the context in Scripture is vital here: it is not simply that the Christian is living in a holy way that honors God (which is important enough), but they are doing it *while they suffer—when others in like circumstances would cut and run.* This juxtaposition does not go unnoticed. People ask, "How?" When most people would start to fall apart, the Christian knows that they are always held in the hand of Christ. When most people are overcome by fear, something gives the Christian the courage to continue to stand. As the world observes this, people will ask, "How can you be this way?"

First Peter 3:15 is God's Word to us, bidding us to always be ready. One of the steady things in life is that it is not steady. Undulation is guaranteed. Chances and changes are stressful, and as for troubles, it is not a matter of *if* they will come, but *when*. But Job said, "For I know that my Redeemer lives, and at the last He will stand upon the earth. And after my skin has been thus destroyed, yet in my flesh I shall see God" (Job 19:25–26).

With such faith, we will be ready to stand. What can the world do to us? It may take our lives, but it cannot take our King because He has defeated the devil and death. And if we are with the King, then we are safe. Even Abraham was ready to sacrifice Isaac, knowing that the Lord would be true to His promise: his son would live no matter what (Hebrews 11:17–19).

But this is no mere call to be courageous. The Lord is actually teaching us how this might happen in our lives. One Lutheran teacher says, "To sanctify [make holy] Christ in our hearts is ever to keep him in our hearts as 'the Holy One.' In order to do this properly we ourselves must be 'holy,' . . . sanctified."[31] From a practical perspective, this means that we keep ourselves from the sin of the world.[32] This doesn't mean we are no longer around temptations to sin (which are everywhere), but it means we do not permit sin to be our captain. We are no longer slaves

---

[31] R. C. H. Lenski, *The Interpretation of the Epistles of St. Peter, St. John and St. Jude* (Minneapolis: Augsburg, 1966), 149.

[32] Lenski, *Epistles of St. Peter*, 150.

to sin (see Romans 6:14). If, however, we give in to sin controlling us, not only will people in the world not ask us about our faith, but they might go the other way and make fun of both us and the God we confess.[33]

At the end of the day, when we conduct ourselves this way, instead of fearing people, Christians reverence Christ instead.[34] Peter H. Davids elaborates on honoring Christ in our hearts:

> The heart is the seat of volition and emotion for Peter, the core self of the person. The call is for more than an intellectual commitment to truth about Jesus, but for a deep commitment to him (cf. 1:22). Christ is to be sanctified as Lord. This does not mean to make Christ more holy, but to treat him as holy, to set him apart above all human authority. This sense is clearly seen in the Lord's Prayer, "Hallowed be thy name."[35]

Indeed, the Early Church Father Clement of Alexandria in referring to 1 Peter 3:15 wrote, "This is just what the Lord's Prayer says: 'Hallowed be your name.'"[36] The Venerable Bede expanded on this point: "What does it mean to sanctify God in your heart if not to love that holiness of his which is beyond understanding, in the innermost depths of your heart? Think what strength to overcome all enemies God gives to those from whose heart his holiness shines forth."[37]

Leave it to Luther, however, to break this down even further. Before we quote Luther, let's consider his basic logic, which is reminiscent of the theology of the cross: God chooses to work through that which would lead a person to say, "God is nowhere to be seen!" Luther's logic goes like this:

---

[33] Lenski, *Epistles of St. Peter*, 150.

[34] Peter H. Davids, *The First Epistle of Peter*, The New International Commentary on the New Testament (Grand Rapids, MI: William B. Eerdmans, 1990), 131.

[35] Davids, *First Epistle of Peter*, 131.

[36] Gerald Bray, ed., *James, 1–2 Peter, 1–3 John, Jude*, Ancient Christian Commentary on Scripture, New Testament XI (Downers Grove, IL: InterVarsity Press, 2000), 104.

[37] Bray, *James, 1–2 Peter*, 105.

Premise 1: God works good through what appears to us as either good or bad.

Premise 2: When we sanctify Christ in our hearts and live in faith, God works good.

Conclusion: Therefore, whatever happens to us, good or bad, affirm God working good.

Luther says, "Therefore this is the procedure: You must sanctify Him in your hearts, says St. Peter; that is, when our Lord God sends us something—whether good or bad, whether it benefits or hurts, whether it is shame, honor, good fortune, or misfortune—I should consider this not only good but also holy."[38] The world will observe you in situations where you could easily give up or run in fear under the circumstances. But instead, you stand firm with objective hope (not subjective wishful thinking), knowing that something *is*, even while not seen. You stand firm because you know God will work good even through suffering the temptation to fear. This is when people ask: "Why do you still have hope?"

One more point: if Christ is indeed holy in us and we are led to live holy lives, then we should ask ourselves, "What exactly do holy lives look like?" Holy lives look like Christians in worship, service, witness, and prayer. If we know of anyone who needs to be engaged for the sake of the Gospel and for their salvation, then let us set apart Christ as holy in our hearts and live in holiness through dedicated prayer for that person. When we pray for someone, we are that much more apt to engage them for Christ. But remember, the first step is living holy lives as we follow Christ and praying for our neighbor so that we are always ready to do the rest of engagement.

What We Are Ready to Say in Engagement

In the context of the considerations above, when anyone asks us to tell them why we have such hope, we are to be ready "to make a defense." It's important that we don't permit ourselves to go from the calmness of

---

[38] AE 30:103.

praying for someone without Christ, to a state of panic when "making a defense" (*apologia*). The idea of making a defense starts to pack the assumption that we must be a powerful orator, possess a litigator's skill, be conversant on the philosophy of religion, and of course, be well versed in the specialized field of Christian apologetics. If we allow all this to fill the definition of "to make a defense," we will run away from engagement.

Let's take a different approach that is entirely biblical while keeping it simple. "To make a defense" is to offer "positive testimony and witness to the truth of the Gospel" (*TLSB*, p. 2155). Such testimony can certainly be developed even with some of the specialized skills mentioned above, but all the Holy Spirit needs to make an impact is for a Christian to give testimony to the truth of the Gospel as he or she might give testimony in the presence of a judge in a court of law.[39]

You're asked, "Why do you have hope?" And you testify, "Because God sent His Son, Jesus Christ, to die to take away the sins of the world and to guarantee eternal life. Because I now know that God is for me, I'm safe!" We should even throw in this: "He died to take away your sins too!" Two things characterize such a testimony:

1. The Christian says it with the conviction that they are telling the truth (because they are)!

2. The Christian backs it up based on the life they live as described above.

That means the Christian substantiates their testimony that the Gospel is truth by the *way they say it* and by the *way they live it*! It's true that the phrase "to make a defense" could be used in a formal way that includes argumentation and the presentation of evidence, but here's the good news for all Christians: it can also be used for informal and personal situations.[40] Such testimony can be used to answer someone who is sincerely seeking hope and truth, and it can also be used to

---

[39] Lenski, *Epistles of St. Peter*, 150.
[40] Davids, *First Epistle of Peter*, 131.

answer someone who is hostile to the faith.[41] Either way, our call is simple: Be ready as you live holy lives for Christ to testify to the truth that Jesus died to forgive the sins of all people, and that this saving work led to Him beating death. He lived for sinners, He died for sinners, and He rose for sinners. Trust in Him, and rest assured that your sins are forgiven. Trust in Him, and know that you have eternal life.

Not Just What You Say, but How You Say It

The conclusion of 1 Peter 3:15 cannot be bypassed. It is just as important as everything else we have considered thus far. Too often, Christians talk down to those who don't know the Gospel. Christians can come off as arrogant people who spend their time judging those they consider to be "sinners." Ironically, Christians—who should by their very name identify themselves as *one who belongs to Christ*—should epitomize not arrogance, but humility.

There are many reasons for the Christian to maintain humility when they engage. One reason is that the Gospel the Christian speaks is the Gospel the Christian needs as much as anyone else. In other words, the Christian does not approach the unbeliever as though the unbeliever is the only sinner in the engagement. On the contrary, since the Christian has a front-row seat to their own sin in their own life, the Christian should be convinced that they are the worse sinner between the two.

A Christian might be able to observe a sin or even many sins in the other person, but how many sins does the Christian observe in themselves? No one can know all their sins (Psalm 19:12), but if we could, how many would that be? A hundred? A thousand? Ten thousand? Indeed, we couldn't count them if we tried. So how on earth can a Christian look down on an unbeliever? It should be a ludicrous impossibility in the minds of all Christians.

The second reason Christians maintain humility is because we have a high responsibility to get it right for God and for the precious person we are engaging with. This person standing in front of you is someone the King of kings lived, died, and rose for. They were created by God and saved by God. They are invaluable to the Lord. If this is

---

41   Davids, *First Epistle of Peter*, 132.

the case, how can the Christian be arrogant during engagement? It should be unheard of.

One more reason to be humble (the third reason): There really aren't just two people in the engagement, but three. The Lord is there. He is in on the engagement. He is there to help lead the Christian, and He is there to help the one without Christ to receive the Gospel in faith (or to do whatever needs to be done for that person at that moment in time; perhaps they need conviction before comfort, for example). Bottom line: The Lord is listening to what the Christian is saying and how they are saying it. We are speaking before God. If this does not make the Christian humble in engagement, nothing will.

St. Peter writes, "Do it with gentleness and respect" (1 Peter 3:15). Luther says that "when you are challenged and are questioned with regard to your faith, you should not answer with proud words and act defiantly . . . you should conduct yourself reverently and humbly, as though you were standing before God's tribunal and had to give an answer there."[42] The ancient teacher Didymus the Blind may have said it best: "Give . . . a proper answer and . . . do so with meekness and in the fear of God. For whoever says anything about God must do so as if God himself were present to hear him."[43]

For all these reasons, we pray for our neighbor and answer them in gentleness, with very great respect toward the Lord, who is with us as we engage. This is what the world needs to see from Christians at a time when the way of the world is to be hostile (even demonizing) toward opponents. The world is anything but humble. But humility is joined to strength when the Christian stands firm in the face of persecution and does not give in to fear or give a defensive or hard answer. Instead, a gentle answer can be offered while giving God reverence. This combination is God's way, and God's way always stands not for pride or hatred, but for the love of the Gospel and those for whom Jesus died and rose.

---

[42] AE 30:108.

[43] Bray, *James, 1–2 Peter,* 104.

CHAPTER 4 DISCUSSION GUIDE

ENGAGEMENT'S APPROACH (1 PETER 3:15)

UNCOVER INFORMATION

1. Who is being addressed in 1 Peter 3:15? Church leaders like pastors and missionaries, or all Christians?

2. What is the first step for engagement?

3. The context of 1 Peter 3:15 teaches that Christians can act differently when times are hard. What does such a life under hardship look like in Christ?

4. When a person allows themselves to be controlled by sin, then what is sin to that person?

5. What two things in 1 Peter 3:15 describe *how* we answer or make a defense?

DISCOVER MEANING

1. What does "make a defense" mean in 1 Peter 3:15?

2. What does it mean to "in your hearts honor Christ the Lord as holy"?

3. Why might an unbeliever ask a Christian about their hope during hard times?

4. What does Romans 6:14 teach about the Christian's relationship with sin? Why is this important for effective engagement?

5. Explain what it means to engage in gentleness and respect. Describe all parties involved.

EXPLORE IMPLICATIONS

1. What's wrong with a Christian saying, "I am not gifted for engagement with the Gospel, so I leave it to others."

2. If we don't take the first step of engagement—honoring Christ as holy in our hearts—then how will attempts for engagement turn out?

3. If God is commanding Christians to be ready to respond as 1 Peter 3:15 teaches, then what might Christians expect to occur in their lives?

4. What are the implications of the logic (two premises and conclusion) based upon Luther's teaching? How should this impact engagement?

5. What will most likely happen if we engage but *don't* do it in gentleness and respect?

CHAPTER 5:
ENGAGEMENT'S ATTITUDE
(1 CORINTHIANS 9:19–23)

Putting Others ahead of Ourselves

Many Christians understand the importance of being constantly faithful to the Word of God. The Christian Church confesses Holy Scripture to be God's inspired and inerrant Word. The Word of God is the greatest gift the Lord has given us on earth. With it—along with the Holy Sacraments—we are kept in the life of Christ. Thus, many Christians understand the importance of *mining* the Word. That is, we aspire to study God's Word for all its worth and continue to draw out its life-giving revelation. In other words, we invest in getting to know the Word of Christ!

At the same time, there is another gift on par with the Word of God that God has also given us: *other people*, especially those people through whom God worked to save our lives or, even more, lead us to eternal life. How important was that parent who sacrificed for you, or that adoptive parent who stepped up when others didn't? How crucial was that teacher who inspired you? How thankful are you for that pastor or other Christian who was there for you during your darkest days? What about that friend who tenaciously pours out God's love upon you? These, too, are God's conduits for knowing Christ.

In his famous *Treatise on Christian Liberty* (*The Freedom of a Christian*), Dr. Luther set forth these two propositions:

1. A Christian is a perfectly free lord of all, subject to none.

2. A Christian is a perfectly dutiful servant of all, subject to all.[44]

Luther was conveying that once a Christian knows the freedom of the Gospel—freedom from the bondage of sin and death—nothing interferes with our new lives in Christ, and in Christ, we have no higher authority. We are, therefore, "subject to none [but God]." At the same time, St. Paul wrote this: "For though I am free from all, I have made myself a servant to all, that I might win more of them" (1 Corinthians 9:19).

This insight should have a profound effect on our understanding of the second point of the engagement triangle: **people**. Our **attitude** is that we shall serve *all* people.

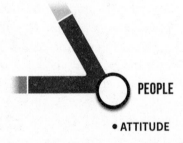

In Christ, we *choose* to be "subject to all." We choose to put others ahead of ourselves. If we are doing it for engagement, however, how important is it that we continue *mining* not only the Word of God *but also the people* God puts in our lives to engage? That is, the Christian is to invest in getting to know people with the same vigor they have for getting to know the Word of Christ.

A great mistake is made when we prioritize the Word but then assume that we should express it the same way to everyone. This is laziness. *While we never change the meaning of Scripture nor "accommodate" people by compromising what Scripture says, we do, however, seek to apply the Scripture in light of the unique person we are engaging.*

---

44 AE 31:344.

An Attitude That Gets into People's Shoes

The Holy Spirit led St. Paul to write what is probably one of the most important Scripture texts on how we approach people for the sake of engaging with the Gospel. It describes the attitude that reaches people for Christ.

> For though I am free from all, I have made myself a servant to all, that I might win more of them. To the Jews I became as a Jew, in order to win Jews. To those under the law I became as one under the law (though not being myself under the law) that I might win those under the law. To those outside the law I became as one outside the law (not being outside the law of God but under the law of Christ) that I might win those outside the law. To the weak I became weak, that I might win the weak. I have become all things to all people, that by all means I might save some. I do it all for the sake of the gospel, that I may share with them in its blessings. (1 Corinthians 9:19–23)

It's true that all people are the same and different at the same time, so when it comes to the engagement attitude, we are focusing on discovering both. The goal should be to capitalize on what is the same. We can speak naturally to this since there is instant common ground. On the other hand, we also want to be aware of what is different. We do this not to be agitated by those differences or to judge them, but rather that we might respect them, even if we cannot understand them or agree with them. By highlighting what is the same and respecting what is different, we can begin to build engagement bridges that demonstrate we value and care about the person we are engaging with.

The best way to do this is by asking questions and then listening very carefully. Indeed, one of the most important things we can possibly do in engagement is active listening. Not *acting* like we're listening but *listening* to optimally get to know the person speaking to us. This means that we take a sincere interest and that we aren't serving an agenda. We are loving them. Our listening says, "You're important to me," and they should be because they are important to God.

When we really listen and learn, we start to relate to the person more and more. This is what we mean by "getting into their shoes." If we get to walk in someone else's shoes, then we have a better idea about the person's life. When this happens, our engagement becomes much more fulfilling and meaningful. It also says the whole time: "I care about *you!*" And we ought to—because God cares about them too!

Being Servant to All

Back in college, I had the privilege of serving on a summer youth ministry team. One of our destinations that summer was Hawaii. When we arrived at our host congregation in Hilo, we were blown away by the amazing feast the people had prepared for us. They insisted, of course, that we be first in line. The food looked so delicious that I think we were all salivating.

I was having difficulty knowing just what to put on my plate when one of our hosts came up to me and said, "Be sure to try the poi." You might know that poi is a Hawaiian dish made from the fermented root of a tropical native plant called *taro* that is baked and pounded into a paste. Poi is a traditional staple of the native cuisine of Hawaii.

Before continuing this story, allow me to insert this subplot: To say I'm a fan of Mexican food would be an understatement. In fact, Mexican food is part of my ethnic heritage. As far as I'm concerned, Mexican food outranks the manna the Lord gave to the Israelites (though I guess I really can't say this since I've never tasted manna). If there was ever any *other* food that came down from heaven, then it's Mexican food. I can't think of a better cuisine, though Chinese comes in a close second. One day I was out with friends and we tried a local Mexican hole in the wall. It had a great reputation. We all ordered these scrumptious-looking plates of Mexican food. I thought the food was outstanding and was jubilant to have discovered this little place. When the waitress came by to get our plates, I hadn't noticed earlier, but my friend sitting next to me *didn't eat his refried beans and Spanish rice*! I can't begin to tell you how much this bothered me. I felt as though he had just slapped me in the face by rejecting some of the delicious staples of my culture! What was wrong with my friend? Did he need counseling or individual absolution or both?

Well, back to Hawaii. I can tell you that as far as I was concerned, just the *look* of the poi was disconcerting. It didn't look right. Consider, however, the circumstances: these gracious hosts had just gone all out to produce this incredible feast. They welcomed us with open arms as we had come to share the Gospel with their Vacation Bible School, which included not only members of the congregation but also people from the community. And finally, one of our generous hosts made it a point to remind me not to forget the poi, which this host seemed especially proud of. She may have made it herself for all I knew.

What was I going to do? Even though I was just a young man at the time, I knew instinctively that we were there to build bridges with people, get to know them, and be in the best possible position to serve them. So, I smiled at my host as I gladly took some poi, and not a modest portion, because I wanted to please my host. I didn't let on to anyone, but when I tasted it, I knew I would do everything in my power to run away as fast as I could if I ever saw poi again. At that moment in time, however, *I ate the poi*, and it built bridges between me and our hosts. I was just praying I wouldn't see it for lunch the next day!

When St. Paul states at verse 19 that he made himself a servant to all, that he might win more of them, Paul was stating his willingness to make personal adjustments for others so that nothing would unnecessarily get in the way of people receiving the Gospel he preached. "The changeless Gospel empowers us to sacrifice our own rights, tastes, interests, and preferences so that others might hear the message of Christ in all its power" (*TLSB*, p. 1958). What was St. Paul really doing? He "showed himself a model of missionary adaptability."[45] This attitude of *adaptability* imitates what our Savior did for us all: "For you know the grace of our Lord Jesus Christ, that though He was rich, yet for your sake He became poor, so that you by His poverty might become rich" (2 Corinthians 8:9). St. Paul had what was an "apparently

---

[45] Gregory J. Lockwood, *1 Corinthians*, Concordia Commentary (St. Louis: Concordia Publishing House, 2000), 314.

chameleonlike stance in matters of social relationships."[46] The Early Church theologian Ambrosiaster was magnificent in his observations:

> Did Paul merely pretend to be all things to all men, in the way that flatterers do? No. He was a man of God and a doctor of the spirit who could diagnose every pain, and with great diligence he tended them and sympathized with them all. We all have something or other in common with everyone. This empathy is what Paul embodied in dealing with each particular person.[47]

St. Augustine states flatly that St. Paul wasn't pretending to be what he was not, but rather, he was showing compassion.[48] He illustrated: "A person who nurses a sick man becomes, in a sense sick himself, not by pretending to have a fever but by thinking sympathetically how he would like to be treated if he were sick himself."[49] Since the Lord Jesus did more than have compassion on us but sympathized to the extent that He took our very sin upon Himself, then what's a little poi?

Four Different Groups of People

St. Paul didn't simply assert that he became a servant of all, but in 1 Corinthians 9:20–22, we learn of how he applied the concept to four different groups of people. Gregory J. Lockwood organizes this invaluable elaboration for us: "Paul now gives four illustrations of how he had adapted his mission strategy to win different people: (1) the Jews (9:20a); (2) those under Law (9:20b); (3) those without Law (9:21); (4) the weak (9:22)."[50]

It might seem that these categories of people are stuck in the past and no longer applicable. Nothing could be further from the truth. True

---

[46] Gordon D. Fee, *The First Epistle to the Corinthians*, rev. ed., The New International Commentary on the New Testament (Grand Rapids, MI: William B. Eerdmans, 2014), 467.

[47] Gerald Bray, ed., *1–2 Corinthians*, Ancient Christian Commentary on Scripture, New Testament VII (Downers Grove, IL: InterVarsity Press, 1999), 86.

[48] Bray, *1–2 Corinthians*, 86.

[49] Bray, *1–2 Corinthians*, 86.

[50] Lockwood, *1 Corinthians*, 311.

to form, the Word of God continues to connect to our contemporary experience. The four groups apply today more than one might think.

The first group: the Jews. The apostle was straightforward in 1 Corinthians 9:20: "To the Jews I became as a Jew, in order to win Jews." Where we begin to see current relevance is not regarding *Jews* per se, but "religious behavior through which the Jews defined their relationship to God" (*TLSB*, p. 1959). In other words, St. Paul was being especially conscientious among people who viewed religion in terms of *keeping the Law.*

To be clear, Law-based salvation puts following the Law *before* salvation, while Gospel-based salvation puts following the Law *after* salvation. The latter is the Christian position. Both groups hold that good works are necessary, but for different reasons. Law-based salvation says the Law must be kept *in order to be saved.* Gospel-based salvation says the Law must be kept *as a result of already having been saved*, where the word *must* does not mean legalistic requirement, but Spirit-led result as in "a good tree bears good fruit" (see Matthew 7:17).

The alarming concern pertaining to the first group (1 Corinthians 9:20) is that no one can do this—achieve salvation through Law-keeping—"for all have sinned and fall short of the glory of God" (Romans 3:23).

With this glaring problem, how in the world did St. Paul "become" a Jew? This was precisely the old religion that St. Paul had left behind. He used to uphold the requirement of circumcision, food laws, and the observance of certain days (*TLSB*, p. 1959). The answer to this question is fantastically important and helps us a great deal.

For the sake of engagement, St. Paul used his freedom in Christ to tolerate and show great patience for the ways of the Jews that he might remain in a position for the Gospel to be made known. "Accordingly, he was careful never to cause them unnecessary offense."[51] As a result, St. Paul sought out public demonstrations to show that he still respected Jewish laws and customs, just *not* for salvation. By doing this, he would

---

51 Lockwood, *1 Corinthians*, 312.

remain in a position to minister also to the Jews without burning bridges that didn't need to be burned.

Contemporary examples aren't hard to think of. What if a Christian was seeking to engage a person who viewed religion in terms of keeping the Law and that this included abstinence from alcohol? Although many Lutherans would be very sad that beer was off the table, the Christian should—in emulation of St. Paul's teaching—be willing to bypass alcohol while sharing a meal with anyone practicing abstinence. Refraining from beer for an entire evening might seem like torture for some, but it is worth it if such consideration leads to the chance to engage. Even one small gesture of deference can cause a relationship to get off on the right foot.

It would be an entirely different situation, of course, if the abstinence signaled condoning the belief that such abstinence contributed to salvation. In such circumstances, the Christian could not in good conscience acquiesce since such thinking denies the Gospel—by grace we are saved through faith in Christ, apart from anything we do (see Ephesians 2:8–9). In this case, go enjoy your brew and toast to the Gospel.

The second group: those under the Law. This group was like the first group, but with a twist: they were not Jews. Instead, these were "the numerous Gentile God-fearers who loved the Jewish people, attended synagogue, and willingly subjected themselves to many aspects of Jewish law."[52] That is to say, they were the same as the first group, but still had differences. St. Paul was consistent in his mode of operation and adjusted whenever he faced anyone in this group as well.

This is helpful because it informs the Christian witness about two truths:

1. In the eyes of God, some things don't matter either way.

2. In the eyes of man, those same things may matter a great deal one way or the other.

---

[52] Lockwood, *1 Corinthians*, 312.

St. Paul was able to remain focused on the Gospel, knowing exactly what was needed and not needed for the Gospel to be the Gospel. But as he brought the Gospel to people, it mattered to know what *they* needed in his conduct so that the Gospel might have free reign.

The third group: those without the Law. Of the four groups, this one might be most applicable to today's culture. This group was without the revelation of God's special Law given to Moses. If we were looking for a contemporary counterpart to this situation, it would be referring to people who are without God's Word in general. While all people—even those without Scripture—have the natural law of conscience, a very large number lack the guiding light of God's Word.

What is it like to have no clue about God's Word? It can lead to a person living life as if they were "the lawless."[53] Because these people do not actually know the Law, "they are not even aware [necessarily] that they are violating it."[54] In the understanding of St. Paul's time, those without the Law would automatically refer to Gentiles (non-Jews), but once again, this was not so much a reference to nationality as it was about people's relationship with the Law.

What happens when the Word of God is a non-factor in a person's life experience? *The Word then—for that person—becomes irrelevant.* As a result, a person learns how to live without it and the more people alive without the Word, the more content they are to keep it that way.

The void in the soul, however, that would have been filled with the Word *must be and will be filled with something else.* It is important to point out that the lack of God's Law does not mean that people are irreligious. In fact, people can be very religious without God's Word, and often they are. But that which fills the void will be a man-made belief system that falls back on *natural religion*, and natural religion is what Luther referred to as *the presumption of righteousness*. Luther wrote, "For as long as the presumption of righteousness remains in a man, there remain immense pride, self-trust, smugness, hate of God, contempt of grace and mercy, ignorance of the promises and of Christ."[55]

---

53 Lockwood, *1 Corinthians*, 309.

54 Lockwood, *1 Corinthians*, 310.

55 AE 26:310.

Notice one of the key descriptors: "self-trust." In other words, natural religion is self-religion where the standards of life are entirely relative and subject to whatever a person feels is right. In this way, when considered from the standpoint of all mankind, nothing is ultimately wrong, and nothing is ultimately right. There is no absolute truth; there is no objective or unchanging truth. At this point, it is easy to stray from God.

In such circumstances, we see why St. Paul would refer to this group as "outside the law" or simply "lawless." And here we go from one extreme to the other: from legalism that demands adherence to the Law, to libertinism that maintains "no law!" Instead of legalism's "*you must do this*," is libertinism's "*do whatever you want*." Both approaches derive from sin against the way of God.

What makes all this fascinating, however, is that St. Paul wrote, "To those outside the law I became as one outside the law" (1 Corinthians 9:21). This is a stunning statement. How can the apostle totally devoted to Christ live as if he were *lawless*?

St. Paul, however, didn't mean that he gave his sinful flesh approval to do whatever it wanted to do. He would have had a hard time with, "When in Rome, do as the Romans do," or, "What happens in Vegas, stays in Vegas." These might make people wink, but St. Paul didn't play games with sin. On the contrary, since he belonged to Christ, his new will led him to renounce rebellion in order to please his Savior and Lord, who gave His life for him.

Still, we haven't gotten to the focus of St. Paul's qualification that enabled him to live with those outside the law. He wrote the rest of 1 Corinthians 9:21: "(not being outside the law of God but under the law of Christ) that I might win those outside the law." What is the "law of Christ"? It is love, and love must serve the neighbor. So, when St. Paul was among the lawless, he held to the law of Christ *to serve them in the best way he could*. This is when a Christian does their service through the free power of the Gospel.[56] St. Augustine wrote, "He did

---

56   R. C. H. Lenski, *The Interpretation of St. Paul's First and Second Epistles to the Corinthians* (Minneapolis: Augsburg, 1963), 379.

this by compassion, not lying. For each one becomes like him whom he wants to help . . . And so he becomes like the other—not by deceiving him but by putting himself in the other's place."[57]

The fourth group: the weak. St. Paul also wrote, "To the weak I became weak, that I might win the weak." Who are "the weak"? Lockwood points out that this designation may have a twofold aspect: (1) weak in the sense of being more easily led into sin; and (2) weak in economic status. Lockwood's elaboration is valuable:

> Most members of the congregation were not well-educated, influential, or of noble birth (1:26–31). Many of them would have worked with their hands for a living. Paul had not held himself aloof from these humble people but had identified with them by taking up his tent-making trade. Thus he exemplified his own maxim, "Do not be haughty, but associate with the lowly" (Romans 12:16).[58]

St. Paul was lovingly condescending as if he were weak by entering into the difficulties of the weak.[59] Ambrosiaster wrote, "Paul became weak by abstaining from things which would scandalize the weak."[60] Indeed, he was always striving to get into people's shoes.

Four "Alls" within 1 Corinthians 9:22–23

You can see St. Paul's emphasis when it comes to people—the attitude toward people—in the engagement triangle: "I have become *all* things to *all* people, that by *all* means I might save some. I do it *all* for the sake of the gospel, that I may share with them in its blessings" (1 Corinthians 9:22–23, emphasis added). Cyril of Jerusalem summed it up for us: "Everywhere the Savior becomes 'all things to all men.' To the hungry, bread; to the thirsty, water; to the dead, resurrection;

---

[57] Bray, *1–2 Corinthians*, 86.

[58] Lockwood, *1 Corinthians*, 313.

[59] Lenski, *St. Paul's*, 379.

[60] Bray, *1–2 Corinthians*, 87.

to the sick, a physician; to sinners, redemption."[61] May this attitude to become all things to all people be ours so that we can truly engage people who are loved by God as much as we are.

---

[61] Bray, *1–2 Corinthians*, 87.

| **CHAPTER 5 DISCUSSION GUIDE** |

ENGAGEMENT'S ATTITUDE (1 CORINTHIANS 9:19–23)

UNCOVER INFORMATION

1. The Word and Sacraments are great gifts to us. What is the other great gift?

2. Should we always express God's Word the same way to all people? Why or why not?

3. What are we trying to accomplish by being aware of the differences we have with people we engage?

4. What kinds of adjustments was St. Paul willing to make in order to more effectively share the Gospel?

5. What were the four different groups of people St. Paul served according to 1 Corinthians 9:20–22?

DISCOVER MEANING

1. What did Luther mean by his two propositions that formed the basis of his famous *Treatise on Christian Liberty* (*The Freedom of a Christian*)?

2. While we want to consider the unique person we are speaking to, and how the Word of God might be presented best to reach them, we do not practice *accommodation*. What is this?

3. What do we mean by "getting into their shoes" for the sake of engagement? Why is this important?

4. What is an attitude of *adaptability* in engagement?

5. In what way did St. Paul become like each of the four groups of people in 1 Corinthians 9:20–22?

EXPLORE IMPLICATIONS

1. How does Luther's teaching on Christian liberty impact the way we view engagement?

2. If we love God's Word and this leads us to *mine it*, what ought we do toward people if we love them (and we strive to engage them)?

3. Why is engagement hurt if we forego discovering common ground?

4. How can being "chameleonlike" be a good and positive thing in engagement?

5. What is the implication of the "alls" in 1 Corinthians 9:22–23 with respect to engagement?

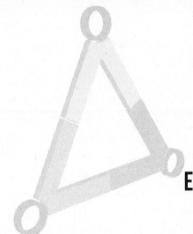

CHAPTER 6:
ENGAGEMENT'S EXAMPLE
(ACTS 17)

The Lutheran Confessions on Acts 17

Smalcald Articles: And God now "commands all people everywhere to repent" (Acts 17:30). "All people," He says. No one is an exception who is a human being.[62]

Formula of Concord, Epitome: God created the body and soul of Adam and Eve before the fall. But He also created our bodies and souls after the fall. Even though they are corrupt, God still acknowledges them as His work. (See . . . Acts 17:28).[63]

Formula of Concord, Solid Declaration: In the article of creation, Scripture testifies that God has created human nature not only before the fall, but that it is God's creature and work also since the fall. (See . . . Acts 17:25). . . .

Therefore, in order that God's creation and work in mankind may be distinguished from the devil's work, we say that it is God's creation that a person has body and soul. Also, it is God's work that a person can think, speak, do, and work

---

[62] SA III III 34.

[63] FC Ep I 4.

anything. For "in Him we live and move and have our being" (Acts 17:28).[64]

The Lutheran Confessions express an extraordinary First Article theology. God is stamped upon everything that exists. He created all things. Given this, all things and especially *people* take on an aura of sanctity when we consider their source. God's concern and His call to repent is not just for *religious* people or for people who go to church. This should have a positive impact on our outlook when it comes to engagement in the world. Because God has created all things and still works through all things, and since Christ died for the sins of the world, we ought to reject the notion that the only response to secular environments is avoidance to the extent that the Gospel would never be spoken.

At the same time, I am not suggesting that we discard wisdom. The Lord Jesus once said, "Do not give dogs what is holy, and do not throw your pearls before pigs, lest they trample them underfoot and turn to attack you" (Matthew 7:6). There are some instances when the environment is so overrun by deliberate and unleashed rebellion against the things of God that the Word of Christ in that environment would be rejected out of hand, and the Christian would become an object of scorn. No, we are not called to be gluttons for punishment.

What kind of environment would this be? Anywhere immorality rules and self-control is gone. When moral restraint flies away and basic dignity is discarded, then the Gospel must be saved for another day. Consider St. Paul's description of "the works of the flesh" in Galatians 5:19–21:

> Now the works of the flesh are evident: sexual immorality, impurity, sensuality, idolatry, sorcery, enmity, strife, jealousy, fits of anger, rivalries, dissensions, divisions, envy, drunkenness, orgies, and things like these.

---

[64] FC SD I 34, 42.

When such things rule a given time and place, then the Holy Spirit has closed the door for engaging with the Gospel. What we should *not* do, though, is mark people involved in such instances and then blacklist them as ineligible for the Gospel. No, Jesus died for them too, and we are to pray for the right time.

The Engagement Triangle: Point 3, Place, Sees the Whole World

With the balanced view of a high First Article theology, while maintaining wisdom about extreme conditions, there is an abundance of opportunities to share the Gospel in the world. Speaking of *world*, let's continue to claim a sacred view of it. While the term *secularism* includes anti-Christian freight (that we will touch on later in this volume), the word *secular* itself simply refers "to the world as it moves in the flux of time."[65] Sproul, Gerstner, and Lindsley observed, "This age may indeed be wicked or paltry, but such negative evaluations only underscore the fact that here is where redemption is needed and is to be applied. In this sense, Christianity is passionately concerned with the secular and the mundane."[66] Thus, the impetus and leaning of the Christian is not to be quick to disqualify the environment from the Gospel, but instead is constantly looking for *ins* so that the light of the Gospel would shine on the darkness.

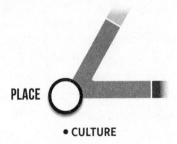

PLACE

• CULTURE

---

[65] R. C. Sproul, John H. Gerstner, and Arthur Lindsley, *Classical Apologetics: A Rational Defense of the Christian Faith and a Critique of Presuppositional Apologetics* (Grand Rapids, MI: Zondervan, 1984), 5.

[66] Sproul, Gerstner, and Lindsley, *Classical Apologetics*, 5.

If we don't affirm this, then our efforts for engagement so that people might know Christ will be over before they begin. We should be leery of the culture's assertion that religion and faith should be practiced at home or at places of worship, but *not in the public square.*[67] The Christian needs to be cognizant that this is real satanic temptation that would program us to zip it up when it comes to the Gospel when we are out and about. What is more, a false sense of piety tries to sneak in to join the bandwagon against engaging in public. We think, "That which is of the Church is holy, but that which is of the world is profane; the two just don't mix." This is going too far. Some commentary on Luther helps here: "But the church must be profane if it is to be the church; profane not in the vulgar sense but in the sense in which Luther used it—that the church must come outside of the temple (*pro fanus*) and into the world."[68]

Sports Bar Amazing Grace

Given the exciting First Article theology of God's Word and the Lord's view of the world that He created and the sins of the world He died for, I was excited when one of my parishioners opened a sports bar. He did so with the intentional vision of bringing the Gospel to a crowd that might not normally be reached by the Gospel. Nothing was spared to make his venture successful: tables conducive for playing cards, a shiny horseshoe bar, booths, a large area outdoors for live music, a smaller stage inside perfect for karaoke, and even billiards. What made it even better was my parishioner's high standard of operations: employees were dressed professionally, anyone having too much to drink turned over their keys, and disruptive conduct was immediately shown the door. We blessed the place at its grand opening.

Though I didn't frequent it often, I went when I could support my parishioner, mindful of the special openings for the Word of God that might be encountered. But if this might happen, then I had to consider the place. As I mentioned above, where moral restraint is lacking, *that*

---

[67] I address this erroneous idea in *Faith That Sees through the Culture,* chapter 9: "The Lutheran Lens—Where Are We?"

[68] Sproul, Gerstner, and Lindsley, *Classical Apologetics,* 6.

is not the time for the Gospel. Even if there were good conditions, I still had to consider how people in the culture would respond to a pastor walking in, especially as I frequently wore my clerical. In fact, I'm fairly certain that *every* time I visited, I had on my clerical collar.

One night I strolled in, eyed an open chair at the bar, noticed that the man sitting next to that chair was *not* unruly, and there went to claim my space. I ordered a beer and said hi to my parishioner's daughter working as a bartender. When the man sitting next to me realized I knew the bartender, he turned a good 45 degrees to get a better look at me. You should have seen the look on his face. When he saw my collar, I think he suddenly had to look around to make sure that *he* was in a sports bar.

I immediately said hi and shook hands with surprised Randy, and we were off to the races. The first point of the engagement triangle gave me **perspective** so that I knew how to **approach**: the Lord had put me there, and the Lord was with me as much in that moment as He was when I was an officiant at the sacred altar during Divine Service. The perspective reminded me that it was God, Randy, and me. Randy would get my gentleness, and the Lord would have my respect.

Next, I considered **people** in order to have the right **attitude** regarding the two people engaging: myself and my new friend Randy. I had to jettison any preconceptions, especially as they might involve people who frequented sports bars in general, and then I needed to view this man as so important that Christ shed His blood for him. No matter our differences, I was called to love him as I loved myself. I was called to have an open heart toward him, not to judge him, and I was to seek whatever we had in common. At this moment in time, Randy and I had the bar in common as well as a friendly introduction.

The third point on the triangle, **place**, led me to think about Acts 17, which I've carried with me for years before writing this book. It has inspired me for as long as I can remember. St. Paul once hung out with the Athenians at the Areopagus just below Athena, patron goddess of the city and goddess of wisdom and war (always an intriguing combination) who, of course, resided in the famed Parthenon, built upon the

Acropolis in Athens, Greece. What might be the best example for Gospel engagement encourages me whenever I venture into unusual places.

The first thing my new friend and I had to get out of the way is how a pastor could be in a bar drinking a beer. This was a great way to break the ice and just have a friendly conversation. I shared a lot with Randy, including why pastors *should be out and about in the world since God loves all people*, and then I went over the four ways alcohol is permitted in God's Word (for celebrations, for the despairing, for medical purposes, and for Holy Communion). The next thing I knew, I was given the chance to tell Randy about Jesus. As a grand finale, the pastor in the clerical collar was invited up for karaoke. What did I sing? "Amazing Grace." And Randy wasn't the only one to hear it. I was emboldened for all of this from St. Paul's example in Acts 17.

The Place Should Move the Heart of the Christian

St. Paul was not sightseeing. He was no tourist. He went to places that had a great need for the Gospel of God. Athens was full of idols and temples, and the Athenians represented a people inundated by idolatry. I've been asked which of the Ten Commandments is most grievous to break. It's a good question, since breaking *any* proves that we are on our own condemned sinners who commit sins. Nevertheless, the First Commandment is not randomly first. It is also the single most important commandment. Get this first one wrong, then everything else will be wrong. "You shall have no other gods. What does this mean? We should fear, love, and trust in God above all things," as Luther says in the Small Catechism.

I mention these things so that we would have an idea of what was going on in St. Paul. There was nothing breezy about this visit to Athens. Acts 17:16 states that "his spirit was provoked within him." St. Paul was upset. It would not be going too far to say that he was angry. Why would he be angry? Because the false gods were set up in the face of the true God. "Scripture sometimes calls this emotion 'jealousy.'"[69] John Stott points out, "Now jealousy is the resentment of rivals, and whether

---

[69] John R. W. Stott, *The Spirit, the Church, and the World: The Message of Acts* (Downers Grove, IL: InterVarsity Press, 1990), 278.

it is good or evil depends on whether the rival has any business to be there."[70] The apostle loved the Lord so much that he resented anything that sought to replace His glory and honor. But further, this visceral reaction is testimony that St. Paul knew how dire the situation was in Athens. He wrote, "What pagans sacrifice they offer to demons and not to God" (1 Corinthians 10:20).[71]

All of St. Paul's senses were piqued; he was sober, he was focused, and he had made an important diagnosis about the place. He was preparing himself to speak to it. And he did speak to it, to the extent that Acts 17:17 informs us he engaged a cross section of people, both Jews and devout people in the synagogue *and* in the marketplace (*agora*). This is an important transition. Notice that he didn't scurry out of town because he was upset. Rather, his provoked spirit inspired a "positive and constructive" response.[72] He was determined to engage the people and not allow the false idols to claim victory.

It is also important to mark the word used here to describe *how* St. Paul spoke to these people. The Word says he *reasoned* with them. The original word could mean "argue," or it could mean simply "discuss" or "converse." Even if he did argue, it must have been in accord with the intelligent use of reason (subservient to God's Word) as opposed to being *argumentative*. At Acts 19:8, the same word is combined with *persuading*, and Acts 19:9 uses the same word to describe a *daily* activity. These descriptors would hardly represent a shouting match, hostile exchanges, or argumentation for pride's sake. St. Paul was really engaging and investing his time into knowing the people there. Paul was not condemning people (even if his spirit had been provoked by the place) but conducting meaningful engagement. The place moved St. Paul not to *abandon* these people, but to *have the energy to pursue them, to give his full attention to them, and to love them.*

---

[70]   Stott, *The Spirit, the Church, and the World*, 278.

[71]   F. F. Bruce, *The Book of the Acts*, rev. ed., The New International Commentary on the New Testament (Grand Rapids, MI: William B. Eerdmans, 1988), 329.

[72]   Stott, *The Spirit, the Church, and the World*, 280.

At the Areopagus

It is one thing to go to the synagogue where fellow Jews were and another thing to venture into the marketplace for adventurous encounters, but the Areopagus? St. Paul was suddenly in a position to engage those in the major leagues, the most prestigious Athenians. This was the high court of Athens where arguments were heard and weighed by the best minds. Not just anyone could address the Athenians at the Areopagus; one had to be invited.[73]

The engagement triangle was in play. St. Paul's **perspective** was solid, as he had dedicated himself to set apart Christ as holy, especially in the face of idols. He had also studied the **people** and was ready to build bridges. And he was cognizant of the **place**, along with its religious and philosophical influences from men and its dark spiritual influences from demons upon the city.

Recall the goal to consider how people are the same and different at the same time so that common ground is recognized and relied upon, even while we try to be aware of differences so that we may respect those we speak to—even if those differences are vast. St. Paul grabbed hold of something he and the Athenians held in common. "So Paul, standing in the midst of the Areopagus, said: 'Men of Athens, I perceive that in every way you are very religious'" (Acts 17:22).

St. Paul was not being patronizing. This wasn't a sale or a pitch; he was dead serious about winning these hearers. He was firm and clear; he was bold yet had "the wisdom of adapting his tone and general approach to the particular audience . . . being addressed at the time."[74] What did they have in common? They both sought to be devoted and very religious. There is debate about the characterization "very religious," but rest assured that *St. Paul was not so dense as to begin his engagement by insulting the Athenians.*

Whether the words are translated as "religious" or "superstitious" or "devoted," this was neither compliment nor insult: it was *fact*. Given that, the opening was courteous[75] and considerate of *what the Athenians*

[73] R. C. H. Lenski, *The Interpretation of the Acts of the Apostles* (Minneapolis: Augsburg, 1961), 719.

[74] Bruce, *Book of the Acts*, 334.

[75] Stott, *The Spirit, the Church, and the World*, 284.

were. What was St. Paul doing? He was respecting them while demonstrating real knowledge about them. At the same time, the apostle was not being misleading, because to be very religious and devout is a general characteristic any true believer should possess. St. Paul's goal was to redirect this characteristic toward the true God.

This is engagement in action. What can be said that demonstrates investment and care for the one you're talking to?

1. Something that says, "Your life is important enough for me to know something about it" straight out of the chute.

2. Something that says, "I can relate to this thing, and so we have something in common."

At this juncture, St. Paul had their attention, but now he needed a hook, or an in. What would really *connect*? He says in Acts 17:23, "For as I passed along and observed the objects of your worship, I found also an altar with this inscription: 'To the unknown god.' What therefore you worship as unknown, this I proclaim to you." This was how St. Paul would be able to eventually include the Gospel into his engagement with the Athenians. Here is the Early Church Father Chrysostom:

> They [the Athenians] certainly wrote that [to an unknown god] with a different meaning, but he [St. Paul] was able to change it . . . For this reason Paul said from the beginning, "I see how extremely religious you are in every way . . . you not only worship the gods who are known to you, but also those who are still unknown to you." Therefore they had written, "To an unknown god." . . . The unknown God is none other than Christ.[76]

---

[76] Francis Martin, ed., *Acts*, Ancient Christian Commentary on Scripture, New Testament V (Downers Grove, IL: InterVarsity Press, 2006), 218.

Some might think that maybe St. Paul was being too hasty and that perhaps his jump to *the hook for the Gospel* came too soon, but there is something else St. Paul did that would have increased his showing of respect and common knowledge of the Athenians. When he said, "What therefore you worship as unknown, this I proclaim to you," the apostle used *neuter*, not *masculine* forms.[77] This buttressed their own admission that they didn't know who the unknown God was. Since the unknown God was unknown, St. Paul was considerate of their understanding (or lack of understanding) in the way the Athenians would have referred to the unknown God. St. Paul was actively *getting into their shoes*.

So, based on the above, what has St. Paul's example taught us about what we should say?

1. Something that says, "What you already know about is a way to know something about God."

2. Something that says, "Let me tell you more about Him."

The "more," of course, is the saving Gospel that in Christ, God has forgiven all people for all sins for all time. Acts 17 provides us an example for considering **place**, the third point of the engagement triangle, so that the Gospel would be even more effective in its transmission. It is now time for us to consider major cultural issues that challenge engagement with the Gospel.

---

[77] Bruce, *Book of the Acts*, 336.

CHAPTER 6 DISCUSSION GUIDE

ENGAGEMENT'S EXAMPLE (ACTS 17)

UNCOVER INFORMATION

1. When should engagement *not* take place?

2. What is the Christian always looking for in their environment? *Ins* for what?

3. "The Church and the world don't mix; therefore, keep faith to yourself." Is this a good view or a bad view? Why?

4. What kind of place was Athens where St. Paul went?

5. What did St. Paul say to the Athenians at the Areopagus as he tried to establish common ground?

DISCOVER MEANING

1. What is our Savior teaching us at Matthew 7:6: "Do not throw your pearls before pigs"?

2. Whereas *secularism* is against the faith, the word *secular* is not a bad word. What does it mean? Why should the Christian be very interested and attentive to it?

3. Luther said, "The church must be profane if it is to be the church." What did he mean?

4. What does it mean that St. Paul's spirit was "provoked" by what he saw in Athens?

5. In what general way did St. Paul truly share common ground with the Athenians who were polytheists and idolaters?

EXPLORE IMPLICATIONS

1. What would happen if we tried to engage with the Gospel in an "environment . . . overrun by deliberate and unleashed rebellion against the things of God"?

2. If faith and religion were confined to personal dwellings and places of worship, what would be wrong with this picture?

3. If the Church is rightly profane (as Luther explained), where should it go?

4. How could St. Paul be provoked in spirit and yet be so inspired to engage the people in Athens?

5. St. Paul's words in Acts 17:23 give us his example for engagement. What was he trying to accomplish?

PART III:

ENGAGEMENT TRIANGLE APPLIED TO CULTURAL ISSUES AROUND US

CHAPTER 7:
ENGAGING SCIENCE

Small Catechism

The First Article: I believe in God, the Father Almighty, Maker of heaven and earth.

What does this mean? I believe that God has made me and all creatures; that He has given me my body and soul, eyes, ears, and all my members, my reason and all my senses, and still takes care of them. He also gives me clothing and shoes, food and drink, house and home, wife and children, land, animals, and all I have. He richly and daily provides me with all that I need to support this body and life. He defends me against all danger and guards and protects me from all evil. All this He does only out of fatherly, divine goodness and mercy, without any merit or worthiness in me. For all this it is my duty to thank and praise, serve and obey Him. This is most certainly true.

Engagement Triangle Point 1: Perspective and Approach

Integration between Faith and Science

The Christian Church confesses the First Article of the Creed, and when she does, she also affirms the created order (the nature of things in accord with the Creator's intent). This order is what science observes, studies, measures, tests, and then categorizes in such a way as to demonstrate its tremendous blessings to humanity. That is, science is a steward, if you will, of God's created order that enables humanity to have better access to and insights about God's First Article gifts.

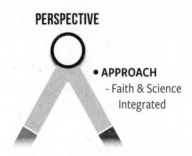

PERSPECTIVE

• **APPROACH**
- Faith & Science
Integrated

Given this, Christians ought to also be *thankful* for the scientific method, which God providentially works through to bless us: observation, formation of hypothesis, testing with data collection, and analyzation, all of which lead to further testing and refinement. In and of itself, *precisely because it emphasizes the study of the created order,* science—consistent with its own methodology—is a great gift from God. "Every good gift and every perfect gift is from above" (James 1:17). In the realm of First Article gifts, has *anything* helped deliver these good gifts to humanity more than science has?

Dr. Gabriela Espinosa (PhD postdoctoral scholar at the University of California, Irvine, biomedical engineering), stated, "Christianity served as part of my motivation to be a scientist. I wanted to understand the created order that I saw in everyday life."[78] Faith seeks understanding, and in approaching science, it *works within the arena of the created order.* Otherwise, what would observation observe and what would experimentation experiment upon? Science is keen to describe that which Christianity considers the foundation of its confession: creation itself.[79]

---

[78] Gabriela Espinosa, interview by the author, Lake Forest, California, January 28 and February 29, 2020.

[79] Alfonso Odilon Espinosa, "Creation," in *The Lutheran Difference: An Explanation & Comparison of Christian Beliefs,* ed. Edward A. Engelbrecht (St. Louis: Concordia Publishing House, 2010), 149. I argue: "Creation and redemption stand or fall together. If the Creator is denied, the true Christ will also be denied." Notice that I have asserted here that creation is the *foundation* of the Christian

Faith seeking understanding, however, does not imply that the Christian faith itself does not have a historical foundation in the tangible world. Dr. Espinosa also shared, "A co-worker once said she was surprised that I was Christian because it's so intangible and we scientists value that which is physical. What a lot of people don't understand is that Christianity *is* tangible and physical! These aren't myths that I choose to believe but historical facts that are not contingent on my belief."[80] Indeed, Dr. Espinosa helps us consider the *historical* nature of the resurrection itself.

The Holy Scriptures do not simply assert that God loves all humanity but reveal what God has done to *demonstrate* His love *in history*. And while it is true that God did this especially when He sent the Christ, it is also true through the ongoing created order. That is, Creator and creation are inextricably linked: "For His invisible attributes, namely, His eternal power and divine nature, have been clearly perceived, ever since the creation of the world, in the things that have been made" (Romans 1:20).

Given this *showing* of God in the created order, the Christian faith celebrates everything that demonstrates the beauty, benefit, and inestimable value of the creation, even in the face of the fallenness of nature that includes death, destruction, and disaster. The difference, of course, is that the good is created by God, while the bad is privation of the good due to sin's entrance into the created order.

From a Christian worldview, therefore, science gives glory (exalted credit) to God by highlighting God's good creation. It therefore stands to reason that science itself—from a Christian worldview—is also a reminder of God's *purpose* for the created order. For the Christian, it speaks to God's love. "The creation is God's arena for giving His gifts of love, especially the gift of His Son."[81]

---

faith. I would also hold that Christology and justification are the *heart* of the Christian faith (most vital teaching) and that the resurrection is the *pivotal event* of the Christian faith. *These three are in classes—among the articles of the faith—of their own.* Without creation, Christianity has no starting point; without justification through Christ alone, Christianity offers no salvation; and without the resurrection, Christianity would have no certainty.

80   Espinosa, interview.

81   Espinosa, "Creation," 119.

Given this, should it surprise us that integration exists between the Christian faith and science? Not since the Christian faith begins with that article that science observes and studies. In fact, history substantiates this integration.

Historians have wondered why modern science arose in the Judeo-Christian West among all world cultures. A good case can be made that the doctrine of creation helped to set the stage for scientific activity. Both Greek and biblical thought asserted that the world is orderly and intelligible. But the Greeks held that this order is necessary and therefore one can deduce its structure from first principles. It is not surprising that they were stronger in mathematics and logic than in experimental science. Only biblical thought held that the world did not have to be as it is, and one has to observe it to discover the details of its order. Moreover, while nature is real and good, it is not itself divine, as many cultures held. Humans are therefore permitted to experiment on nature.[82]

All of this should dispel the assumption held by some Christians that science is antithetical to the Christian faith.[83] Donald M. MacKay helps explain the relationship between faith and science when he points out that in discussing anything, there are different *levels of description of reality*, and these are important if we are going to be thorough "to express all that truthfully needs to be said about it."[84]

This can be demonstrated in discussing—for example—anthropology. Christian faith is intensely interested in *biblical* anthropology, be it regarding the condition of the soul, the expression of the physical, and the practice of the community. *Scientific* anthropological considerations also have much to say relating to human composition via chemistry and biology, or subjective and relational experience via sociology and

---

[82] James E. Huchingson, comp., *Religion and the Natural Sciences: The Range of Engagement* (Fort Worth, TX: Harcourt Brace College Publishers, 1993), 18.

[83] Huchingson, *Religion and the Natural Sciences*, 6. There are, in fact, four major positions about the relationship between faith and science: (1) conflict; (2) independence; (3) dialogue; and (4) integration. The position advocated in traditional Christianity is integration, especially demonstrated by the history of science in which so many leading scientists were, in fact, Christian.

[84] Donald M. MacKay, *The Clockwork Image: A Christian Perspective on Science*, Christian Classics Series (Leicester, UK: InterVarsity Press, 1997), 90.

psychology. MacKay reminds us, "When properly disciplined, these [faith and science] are not rivals, but complementary, in the sense that each reveals an aspect which is there to be reckoned with, but is unmentioned in the other."[85] He calls this relationship *complementarity* as the different levels of description presuppose the other while revealing the significance of each "in fresh categories."[86]

Why is this important? Dr. Espinosa provided an illustration as to how two aspects can be entirely joined and unified while remaining completely distinct and separate. Frankly, when she provided this picture, I thought of an analogy in sacred theology describing Christ's two natures (divine and human): iron and fire. The fire surrounding the super-hot iron is not iron, and the iron is not the fire. And yet in this instance, they are inextricable. Dr. Espinosa's illustration not only asserts that the two aspects are joined, but that they are also synergistic:

> Cartilage and meniscus are two parts of the knee that are important in the transmission of loading as we go about our day (think shock absorbers). On the macro scale, they are in contact. It's clear on the macro scale that they are distinct and remain so as the joint moves. That is, it is evident that these appear to be clearly separate. The interface between the two looks clean and clear.

> However, when you zoom in to a more micro scale, you'll see that the surfaces of these two structures are not so smooth, therefore, leading to a much larger number of interactions than one would have guessed. You can think of it like interlocking or interdigitation, but it's definitely not mixing. Because these surfaces do have asperities (each of which increase surface interactions), that's going to lead to some increased friction. In the case of the knee joint, the cartilage and meniscus surfaces are lubricated to smoothen the interaction between the two.[87]

---

85   MacKay, *The Clockwork Image*, 90.

86   MacKay, *The Clockwork Image*, 91.

87   Espinosa, interview.

This illustration of *interlocking and yet distinct* approaches the biblical revelation of a unified body and soul that are nevertheless distinct. Science can examine the one; faith can develop the other. Their unity, however, comprises one person. When Dr. Espinosa described the knee, I thought of the person. The interlocking cartilage and meniscus reminded me of body and spirit. The lubrication might stand for what Acts 17:28 says about people with unified body and spirit: "In Him we live and move and have our being."

But let's go further here: can the cartilage affect the meniscus or vice versa? Can the body affect the spirit? Can the spirit have an impact on the body? From the standpoint of biblical theology, there is little doubt that these interact as a system. A spirit bent on destruction can wreck the body. Stress can raise cortisol, and being "scared to death" is not always just a metaphor. On the other hand, a peaceful spirit might lower the heart rate, hope can often increase physical endurance, and God's righteousness through faith can impact the way a person sleeps or copes with anger as both these can easily affect physical health.

And why shouldn't these things hold? "The story of the Bible [to which faith clings] is embedded in history—in reality, the same reality, ultimately, to which natural science speaks."[88] But if this is the case, then why do we so often hear about arguments between faith and science?

Both Theology (That Informs Faith) and Science Have Limitations

If there was one thing my blessed professor back in my graduate course Science and Christianity drummed into us was to remember that, as fields of discipline, both science and theology (the teaching that faith holds to) have their respective limitations. To forsake this one truth was to become susceptible to all kinds of problems.[89] To be sure, many

---

[88] Paul Nelson and John Mark Reynolds, "Young Earth Creationism," in *Three Views on Creation and Evolution*, ed. J. P. Moreland and John Mark Reynolds, Counterpoints (Grand Rapids, MI: Zondervan, 1999), 56.

[89] John Bloom, "Science and Christianity" (lecture, Biola University, La Mirada, CA, Spring 2000). Dr. John Bloom, academic director for MA in science and religion, Biola University, has two earned doctorates: a PhD in physics from Cornell University and a PhD in Ancient Near Eastern studies from the Annenberg Research Institute (now the Center for Judaic Studies of the University of Pennsylvania).

(if not most) of the so-called *conflicts* between faith and science come as a result of violating this basic principle.

Science has empirical limitations to what can be sensed, observed, and conceived; and even its conclusions are not necessarily absolute. In addition, science is confronted by the challenge of repeatability in experimentation (though repeatability is *a real goal* in science). These limitations, however, are not unique to science and describe the human experience in many fields, indeed, even in day-to-day experience. Just think of someone who establishes that the route between house and work takes x amount of time to traverse. The only problem is that x comes out with significant variations for many reasons.

At the same time, there are also limits in Christian theology. Interpretation of the biblical texts must bridge the gap of culture and language, and these represent a degree of historical limitation. In addition, Holy Scripture nowhere claims to be a scientific textbook and shows relatively little interest in mechanical explanations of the physical world. To be sure, many of the results of revelation can only be borne out over time, and often well beyond a person's lifetime.[90] Nelson and Reynolds remind us that "just as Scripture is dependent on a hermeneutic for understanding, so science is dependent on an interpretive framework for comprehensibility."[91]

Given this situation, what happens when limitations are ignored? What occurs is that the two fields themselves can be compromised in the way they are expressed and presented. When this happens, the integrity of that field unnecessarily suffers *when the practice of the discipline fails to stay within the parameters of the discipline itself.*

Why do Christians sometimes go too far? Often on account of wrong assumptions about what God gives us to do. This book is about engagement because God has in fact,

1. provided the **perspective** that God has called us to set apart Christ as Lord in our hearts as holy and to be prepared to give

---

90   Bloom, lecture Spring 2000.

91   Nelson and Reynolds, "Young Earth Creationism," 71.

testimony about the hope within us with gentleness and respect (1 Peter 3:15);

2. called us to serve the **people** who remind us of the need for becoming all things to all men so that through all means some might be saved (1 Corinthians 9:22); and

3. led us to consider the **place** as was considered when St. Paul was at the Areopagus, fully aware of the unique circumstances of his environment (Acts 17:22–31).

What is not on this list? For one, *trying to prove that the Christian faith is 100 percent absolutely true.*[92] Conversion does not depend on a comprehensive presentation of historical facts, be they more or less theological or scientific, but on the faithful transmission of the Gospel of Christ. Through the Word of Christ, the Holy Spirit brings hearers to know the love of Christ. For this reason, we properly confess that it is only the Holy Spirit who converts anyone.

Timothy Keller explains, "Despite all the books calling Christians to provide proofs for their beliefs, you won't see philosophers doing so, not even the most atheistic."[93] Of course, one can almost always find an exception, but Keller's point is well taken. He goes on, "The great majority [of philosophers] think that strong rationalism is nearly impossible to defend.[94] To begin with, it can't live up to its own standards."[95]

---

[92] Consider 2 Corinthians 10:5: "We destroy arguments and every lofty opinion raised against the knowledge of God, and take every thought captive to obey Christ." That is, Christians might employ negative apologetics to demonstrate the weaknesses of arguments that attack the faith, and positive apologetics to testify to evidences that point to and resonate with the truthfulness of the faith. However, none of this is the same as telling someone, "I can demonstrate to you that the Christian faith is true beyond a shadow of a doubt." In the same way, no one else—atheist, other world-religionist, skeptic, or secularist—can maintain their positions based on strong rationalism either.

[93] Timothy Keller, *The Reason for God: Belief in an Age of Skepticism* (New York: Riverhead Books, 2009), 122–23.

[94] "Strong rationalism" is the belief that something can be shown to be true in a way that is convincing to *any* reasonable person.

[95] Keller, *Reason for God*, 123.

But this is not to say that some folks—coming from both faith and science—don't *try* to speak in terms of absolute proof.[96]

What happens when Christians cross the line? Not only are they trying to usurp what only God the Holy Spirit can do and convince someone that the faith is true, but just as troublesome, the Christian also gives up on faith itself. "Now faith is the assurance of things hoped for, the conviction of things not seen" (Hebrews 11:1). But this does not mean that faith is based on rationalistic proof. In other words, Christians arrive at absolute certainty—in accord with the new creation, not the sinful flesh that always disbelieves—on account of the Holy Spirit through faith, not on account of rationalistic arguments. At the same time, even with the most brilliant reasons to trust in Christ, a person will not come to faith without the Holy Spirit.

On the other hand, what if someone tries to treat *science* in an absolutist manner? For one thing, an inaccurate dichotomy will be transmitted: those who advocate science hold to objective evidence, while anyone who confesses faith is ruled by blind subjectivism. This is a disturbing claim, to say the least, and does not follow basic logic. In *Making Sense of God*, Keller outlines: "To state that there is no God *or* that there is a God . . . necessarily entails faith."[97] Furthermore, "No one can purge him- or herself of all faith assumptions and assume an objective, belief-free, pure openness to objective evidence."[98] This is an important insight because at the end of the day, everyone—even someone who says "I don't believe in anything"—operates with faith or "belief." In the same way, both theism and atheism are theological positions requiring faith. Christianity does too, and while it resonates with the rest of what we see in an elegant way, only the Holy Spirit can convince a person that it is true.

When this basic insight is neglected, people can get mean and nasty. Christians can sometimes start to demonize skeptics and atheists, and when they do, the love of Christ for people is left behind. Those who reject the Christian faith can easily do the same. Richard Dawkins

---

[96] Note that there is a difference between absolute truth and absolute proof.

[97] Timothy Keller, *Making Sense of God: An Invitation to the Skeptical* (New York: Viking, 2016), 35.

[98] Keller, *Making Sense of God*, 36.

claims that Christian faith is "blind trust," in the absence of evidence, even in the teeth of evidence.[99] Dawkins's caricature is not the Christian definition of faith, but one that he uses to serve his narrative to discredit faith.[100] The final result of such anti-faith narratives is to view faith as sheer fiction and superstition, having forsaken all rationality and logic. Historical evidence for the resurrection of Jesus Christ, for example, is dismissed out of hand.

Of course, not everyone who rejects Christianity speaks against it in demeaning ways. Many, however, will keep the faith at arm's length by insisting that the two realms have nothing to do with each other. That is, the *complementarity* described above is rejected. But what does this have to do with limitations?

The problem here goes the other way: by forcing *total* separation between faith and science, any benefit the one might have transmitted to the other is lost. That is, limitation in this case is a matter of *depriving fuller knowledge*. Stephen Jay Gould—who was at least agnostic—advocated what is known as *non-overlapping magisteria* (NOMA) that keep faith and science far apart. "On Gould's view, the 'magisterium of science' deals with the 'empirical realm,' whereas the 'magisterium of religion' deals with 'questions of ultimate meaning.'"[101] This, however, is a caricature of faith, as many religionists would assert that their faith very much contributes to their empirical or experiential lives. Unfortunately, when total separation is insisted upon, potential beneficial integrations are cut off.

Still, Christians mustn't relish criticism against atheists, for example, and lose humility. The fact is that sometimes Christians covet science more than they should when it comes to biblical interpretation, and once again, limitations are breached. This can happen even when strong rationalism is rejected. In other words, science might begin to be used to *interpret* Scripture. This is more than possible, especially in consideration of this principle offered by St. Augustine:

---

[99] Alister McGrath and Joanna Collicutt McGrath, *The Dawkins Delusion? Atheist Fundamentalism and the Denial of the Divine* (London: SPCK, 2007), 1.

[100] McGrath and McGrath, *The Dawkins Delusion*, 1.

[101] McGrath and McGrath, *The Dawkins Delusion*, 18.

First, the truth of Scripture must be held inviolable. Secondly, when there are different ways of explaining a Scriptural text, no particular explanation should be held so rigidly that, if convincing arguments show it to be false, anyone dare to insist that it still is the definitive sense of the text. Otherwise unbelievers will scorn Sacred Scripture, and the way of faith will be closed to them.[102]

We are aware of the historical context of this view as Lindberg and Numbers highlight: "These two vital points constituted the basic medieval guidelines for the application of a continually changing body of scientific theory and observational data to the interpretation of physical phenomena described in the Bible."[103] Simply put, science might hone biblical interpretation.

While St. Augustine is one of the most important Christian theologians who ever lived, his counsel, in this case, could be as dangerous as it is helpful. That is, the principle could be taken too far. There are some things in the Christian faith that are beyond *any* scientific explanation that we know of. No scientific explanation has been identified, for instance, that explains the bodily resurrection of the Lord Jesus Christ. Not one. But suppose someone came along and said that the bodily resurrection of Christ is not substantiated by science, so there is reason to doubt it. The person then said that we should therefore reject the traditional confession of the resurrection, given St. Augustine's dictum that I should consider "convincing arguments" about Christ's resurrection with better explanatory power (e.g., spiritual resurrection, existential resurrection, it was not Christ on the cross at all, He never actually died, etc.). In this case, Augustine's dictum, for all its allurement, is something orthodox Christianity would be compelled to reject out of hand.

Now St. Augustine did not doubt the bodily resurrection of Christ, but as for his dictum, we must be aware that a person might try too

---

[102]   David C. Lindberg and Ronald L. Numbers, eds., *God and Nature: Historical Essays on the Encounter between Christianity and Science* (Berkeley, CA: University of California Press, 1986), 63.

[103]   Lindberg and Numbers, *God and Nature*, 63.

hard to apply it. So, three things are concluded here regarding this section on faith and science:

1. Faith and science have their respective limitations.

2. When limitations are ignored, both fields are compromised.

3. Compromise can go the direction of either too much separation or too much convergence between the two fields.

Sometimes Conflict Seems Inevitable

The age of the earth and the historicity of Genesis 1–11 are examples of controversy surrounding faith and science. These are so controversial, in fact, that we must carefully weigh how much these should be pursued during engagement for the Gospel. This is not to say that these aren't vitally important issues.[104] The *reason* for their tremendous import relates directly to our handling of the Holy Scriptures, and what is particularly at issue is *whether the traditional view that treats especially Genesis 1–11 as actual history is correct and true.*

As the traditional view of six consecutive twenty-four-hour days has been questioned, other views, of course, have been put forth. These include progressive creationism, framework hypothesis, Genesis as myth, Schroeder's two frames of reference, and, of course, what is probably the most popular alternative: theistic evolution. In light of these, if anyone tries to maintain six consecutive days (not necessarily twenty-four hours), then they might use the day-age theory, where each "day" equals an epoch of time. They may also use the gap theory, where there is a very long gap of time between Genesis 1:1 and 1:2, or they may view the consecutive days as conveying an orderly creation without reference to time at all.

For many Christians, this is a non-issue, as they have comfortably turned from the traditional interpretation of six consecutive twenty-four-hour days. The issue, however, is not merely about "days," but has

---

[104] So important, in fact, that I defended the six days of creation as actual consecutive twenty-four-hour days in *The Lutheran Difference*, 131–36.

deeper implications with respect to the historicity of the Scriptures and demonstrates that the traditional view has a wrong way of reading Genesis 1–11. These are serious alternatives so that those who hold to the traditional view might share this perspective from Nelson and Reynolds: "It is always safest to agree with the spirit of the age. But it is not always best."[105] But why do so many Christians hold to the traditional view?[106]

Jesus clearly regarded the account of Adam and Eve's creation as factual, as well as the flood. He affirmed many people and events of the past that skeptics deny ever existed or happened: Adam and Eve (Matthew 19:3–6; Mark 10:2–9), Abel (Luke 11:51), Noah and the flood (Matthew 24:37–39; Luke 17:26–27), Abraham (John 8:56–58), Sodom and Gomorrah (Matthew 10:15; 11:23–24), Daniel (Matthew 24:15), Jonah and the great sea creature (Matthew 12:39–41).[107]

In addition, "In the New Testament, there are over 100 quotations from or allusions to Genesis 1–11, none of which hints at Genesis being anything other than history."[108]

But having said all this, let's say that a Christian could convince someone without faith in Christ that the Word of God was inspired and inerrant and that Genesis 1–11 was historical narrative describing actual history. These things—as sacred as they are to the Christian faith—would not in themselves lead a person to saving faith in Christ. Only one thing does that: namely, the Gospel. Without the knowledge and trust that one's sins are forgiven through Christ, and without understanding and holding to Christ's resurrection as our release from eternal death, nothing else will save a person's life from sin and death.

Given this, how much should we turn our engagement into a debate about the age of the earth? How much should we argue the historicity of Genesis 1–11 with someone who has never heard the Gospel? I'm not at all saying that these things should not be argued with all theological

---

[105] Nelson and Reynolds, "Young Earth Creationism," 96.

[106] As held by The Lutheran Church—Missouri Synod.

[107] Robert J. M. Gurney, *Six-Day Creation: Does It Matter What You Believe?* (Leominster, UK: Day One, 2007), 26.

[108] Gurney, *Six-Day Creation*, 29.

rigor, but as the saying goes, *there is a time and place for everything*, and engagement for the Gospel is probably not that time and place. Is this disingenuous? It would be only if we were dishonest. If the one with whom we are engaging were to ask us about Genesis 1–11, we should not be deceitful, but honest: "As important as that subject matter is, have you ever heard about the Christ prophesied and the fulfillment of those prophecies? Have you heard about what God has done about our shame and death?" That's not disingenuous. That's prioritizing.

Engagement Triangle Point 2: People And Attitude

What All People Have in Common regarding Faith and Science

Dr. Roderick Soper has a PhD in science education from Curtin University of Technology in Perth, Western Australia, and is a professor of biology at Concordia University, Irvine. He cut to the chase when we spoke about what is probably the Christian's best and most reliable point of contact and commonality with anyone holding to science as indispensable to their worldview.[109]

I smiled when Dr. Soper said right off the cuff, "Jesus' ministry was evidential, but He wasn't out to prove anything." These were bold words to start with, words that some Christian apologists might even find scandalous, but he was restating my position.

PEOPLE

- **ATTITUDE**
  - Neither Faith nor Science Assert Absolute Proof

---

[109] Roderick Soper, interview by author, Lake Forest, California, November 5, 2019.

People don't live their lives considering everything they do and everything they basically believe as that which must be proven. It just doesn't happen. With exception of obviously flimsy chairs, no one conducts experiments on every chair they sit on for indisputable proof that each collection of atoms in the shape of a chair will actually sustain their weight. We eat the food from drive-throughs and don't typically ask the managers for proof that their food safety certificates are up to date. We ask our virtual assistants for the temperature outside, but we don't follow up by walking out into the backyard with a thermometer to verify their reports. When my dog comes into my study wagging her tail, and, with a low growl-groan, tries to tell me something, chances are she needs to go out to do her thing. I've never misread her once. The examples that we live this way are endless.

As Dr. Soper says, *all* people share this process. It is a universal mode of operation, and what is more, it is a process that exerts what he also refers to as *probabilistic thinking*. It doesn't matter who you are—scientist or theologian, rich or poor, young or old, Laker or Celtic fan (though Celtic fans might need more grace), student or professor—we all operate in like manner.

But the similarities don't end there. The split second we realize we operate *probabilistically*, we also realize that such living *requires a real acceptance of uncertainty*. But that's okay, because even while we are *not*, in fact, 100 percent certain about something, we can gather data that might be consistent with what we know, have seen, and have experienced about that thing. When mounting evidence—without absolute proof—resonates with actual experience, a person begins to form real probabilistic buy-in or at least a genuine openness to hear the Gospel.

Are scientists any different? They, like the rest of humanity, work moving along evidentiary baselines—and hopefully, if they are considering the Christian faith, they move from "I don't know" toward "I know" by discovering what is increasingly probable as the engaging Christian gently shares their testimony about the hope that is in them. If empirical and relational evidence continues to mount, buttressed by engagement with the Gospel, faith may very well come as the Holy Spirit gifts it.

The Lord Jesus fits in such an approach. We might say to the one we engage with who does not know Christ, "So, there is much you don't know about Christ? That's okay. But know this: Christ identified Himself *with* truth. In fact, Jesus said, 'I am the way, and the truth, and the life' (John 14:6). Do you need to consider His claim probabilistically? Good. Consider His life: He lived a life of love, and He was a real Savior who loved real people in real history." He was no "value judgment" (as Dr. Soper points out) or mere idea, but He is epitomized by His enduring Scriptures *and* His living representatives. Both broadcast His love and can be experienced. The scientific method can begin *here*! If a scientist who does not know the Gospel gets enough of that empirical exposure, combined with engagement for the Gospel, they may very well begin to believe.

It might seem that we have made a leap to go from Christ during His public ministry two thousand years ago to the "empirical exposure" of the Christian faith today, but a tangible bridge exists in the space-time continuum. Between Christ two thousand years ago and His Church today is a real history marked by a real tradition handling real Scriptures taught, studied, and practiced throughout the history of Christendom. Two things come out here: (1) a stable canon of Scripture that has been remarkably preserved over time, and (2) a stable way of life among the people of God living over that expanse of two millennia that springs from the teaching that has remained constant for centuries.

It's important to address a skeptical claim at this juncture: *Christianity becomes whatever current interpreters make it to be.* With respect to core and basic Christianity, nothing could be further from the truth. For how long has the Church practiced Holy Baptism and Holy Communion? How long has the Church confessed the Ten Commandments, the Creed, and the Lord's Prayer? How long has the Church expounded upon the vital elements of grace, faith, hope, and love? When did the teaching on the necessity of forgiveness begin and end? Has the conviction of the faithful to pray, serve, witness, and worship just occurred in recent history? All these things have been exceedingly stable throughout history. So—once again—two things have endured: (1) the source of teaching, and (2) the way of life. Both these invite empirical scrutiny.

Dr. Gabriela Espinosa reinforced Dr. Soper's relational and experiential emphasis that bears out Scripture and life: "I think this goes back to the desire to do good. My conversations with fellow scientists about the awesome work that the Church does to help those in need has resonated with them so well. I've even invited some to come volunteer with me and have gotten positive responses. It's great when we, Christians, can lead efforts that everyone can get on board with, such as food banks, after-school programs, and visits to the elderly. These are the things Christians and scientists (and those who are both) can do together!"[110] Scientists observe. What will they observe from those who bear the name of Jesus? If we are faithful, the historic confession flowing from the Scriptures and the life of Christ will speak for itself and engagement will be bold to speak of what Jesus did for all people and demonstrate the empirical life that flows from the Gospel.

This is our common ground with people:

1. We all think probabilistically.

2. We all have a real acceptance of uncertainty (not including faith itself, Hebrews 11:1).

3. So, we look for real experiences, empirical evidence, that moves us along the continuum from "I don't know" to "I know," as the claims of Christianity touch scientists when the love of Christ is seen to be taught in Scripture and demonstrated in our lives.

Engagement Triangle Point 3: Place and Cultural Influence

Timothy Keller points out: "'A *secular age*' is one in which all the emphasis is on the *saeculum,* on the here-and-now, without any concept of the eternal. Meaning of life, guidance, and happiness are understood and sought in present-time economic prosperity, material comfort, and emotional fulfillment."[111] This is the culture's influence upon the

---

[110] Espinosa, interview.

[111] Keller, *Making Sense of God*, 3.

engagement between faith and science. It is demonic as it tries to make life devoid of God and the Christian faith devoid of relevance. At the same time, the external things of culture attempt to make science the extension of a self-serving worldview that would like the Christian faith to disappear.

Such influences claim that faith is superstition and the direct opposite of science, which alone—according to this view—is objective and trustworthy in the eyes of cultural extremists. These also seek to disrupt integration between faith and science, so that eventually science might stand alone. When science does stand alone, under these circumstances, its limitations are violated so that science begins to say more than it is qualified to say. Such circumstances put Christians on the defensive, and before long, Christians are tempted to try to *prove* that Christianity is true rather than engage for the Gospel. When this happens, Christians can begin to turn from faith so that faith is replaced with the unattainable goal—apart from the Holy Spirit—of absolute certainty. Even worse, the Christian might stop loving their neighbor, replacing gentleness and respect with arguments and combativeness.

PLACE

• **CULTURE**
- Resist Either-Or Mentality

What is the Christian to do under such circumstances? First, set apart Christ the Lord as holy in the heart, be gentle toward the neighbor, and reverence God as you engage. Second, affirm the integration of faith and science, know that these are from God, see the benefits of their complementarity, and give thanks to God for these as *gifts* to us. Christians can recognize science as that which gives glory to God as it sheds light on His marvelous creation. With this clarity, the

Christian can confidently engage the advocate of science who does not know the Gospel.

Science is not the enemy; sin, the world, and the devil are trying to make us repulsed by science or live in fear in the face of science. Let us instead hold to the gift from God that is science so the world sees that not only do Christians *not* run from science, we embrace it, because science helps us to say with the psalmist: "The heavens declare the glory of God, and the sky above proclaims His handiwork" (Psalm 19:1). Science focuses on the heavens, and faith focuses on the Creator, who lives in relation to us in the person of the Christ. We hold to both these in complementarity.

CHAPTER 7 DISCUSSION GUIDE

ENGAGING SCIENCE

UNCOVER INFORMATION

1. What is the scientific method?

2. What part of the Small Catechism relates to the scientific method? In what way?

3. *Why* did God create? From this vantage point, we might say that science helps us to see this even more!

4. Why don't we have to worry about trying to prove the Christian faith?

5. What is probabilistic thinking?

DISCOVER MEANING

1. What is meant by the term *created order*?

2. How is Christianity "tangible and physical"?

3. What do we mean that faith and science are *integrated*?

4. What is strong rationalism, and why is it inappropriate for either faith or science?

5. What is the problem with our *secular age*, and how does it use "science" beyond its limitations?

EXPLORE IMPLICATIONS

1. How did the Christian faith of Dr. Gabriela Espinosa motivate her to be a scientist? In this vein, how does science serve faith?

2. If Creator and creation are inextricably linked, and if science studies and measures the creation, then what is the relationship between Creator and science?

3. What happens if we ignore the limitations of science and Christian theology (which inform faith)?

4. If a person says they have no faith or don't "believe" in faith or religion, does this mean that they are irreligious and faithless? Why or why not?

5. If a Christian gives in to the temptation to try to *prove* Christianity, how will engagement for the sake of the Gospel be compromised?

CHAPTER 8:
ENGAGING POLITICS

Small Catechism

The Fourth Commandment: Honor your father and your mother.

What does this mean? We should fear and love God so that we do not despise or anger our parents and other authorities, but honor them, serve and obey them, love and cherish them.

Table of Duties, Of Civil Government: Everyone must submit himself to the governing authorities, for there is no authority except that which God has established. The authorities that exist have been established by God. Consequently, he who rebels against the authority is rebelling against what God has instituted, and those who do so will bring judgment on themselves. For rulers hold no terror for those who do right, but for those who do wrong. Do you want to be free from fear of the one in authority? Then do what is right and he will commend you. For he is God's servant to do you good. But if you do wrong, be afraid, for he does not bear the sword for nothing. He is God's servant, an agent of wrath to bring punishment on the wrongdoer. Rom. 13:1–4

Augsburg Confession

> Therefore, our teachers, in order to comfort people's consciences, were constrained to show the difference between the authority of the Church and the authority of the State. They taught that both of them are to be held in reverence and honor, as God's chief blessings on earth, because they have God's command. . . . The Church's authority has its own commission to teach the Gospel and to administer the Sacraments [Matthew 28:19–20]. Let it not break into the office of another. Let it not transfer the kingdoms of this world to itself. Let it not abolish the laws of civil rulers. Let it not abolish lawful obedience. Let it not interfere with judgments about civil ordinances or contracts. Let it not dictate laws to civil authorities about the form of society.[112]

Engagement Triangle Point 1: Perspective and Approach

Christian Experience in the Civil Realm

The state is a good thing. God has established the civil government and authorities (Romans 13:1–7; 1 Peter 2:13–14). Even when what is produced seems immoral or unjust, God works through what He has established and works good for His people (Romans 8:28; 10:17). God doesn't need peace in the valley among people to conduct His will and work. For the Christian, this means maintaining the distinction between horizontal and vertical peace. Among people in the culture (the horizontal plane), Christians lack peace (Matthew 10:34), but from the vertical perspective between God and those who know God's grace, they have peace with God (John 14:27; Philippians 4:4–7).

---

[112] AC XXVIII 4, 12–13.

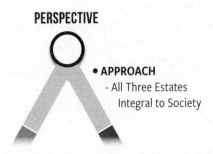

PERSPECTIVE

• APPROACH
- All Three Estates
  Integral to Society

But since the world is not friendly toward those who follow Christ, the Lord was sure to teach His followers: "My kingdom is not of this world" (John 18:36a), and perhaps just so that His Church would not miss the point, He reiterated, "My kingdom is not from the world" (John 18:36b). Given this sobering insight, St. Peter was led by the Spirit of God to write to the dispersed "elect exiles"—those dispersed and struggling Christians needing perspective about life in the world: "Beloved, I urge you as sojourners and exiles to abstain from the passions of the flesh, which wage war against your soul" (1 Peter 2:11). By turning from their own sin, Christians would be less engulfed by the sins of the world. In this way, as the Holy Spirit led God's people—always through the faith-generating and sustaining Word of Christ—Christians would retain their identity and status in Christ. But this retention of Christian identity comes at a price. Stanley Hauerwas and William Willimon are straightforward: "The image of resident aliens [consider 1 Peter 2:11 stated above] means in a possibly offensive way that American Christians need to stop feeling at home."[113] Indeed, the fact that Christians *must* live in this uncomfortable state can tempt even the most devout to feel a little resentful about the way of God, but there is reason to take heart.

God still works on the horizontal plane for His people. In the Old Testament, we see that God appointed the Persian King Cyrus to deliver Israel back to the Promised Land. In so doing, the Lord referred to Cyrus as "My shepherd" (Isaiah 44:28) and "[God's] anointed"

---

[113] Stanley Hauerwas and William H. Willimon, *Where Resident Aliens Live: Exercises for Christian Practice* (Nashville, TN: Abingdon Press, 1996), 24.

(Isaiah 45:1). While we can't be certain about Cyrus's religion, history attests to his political strategy that included honoring the religions of his subjects (as he did toward Israel). But in the eyes of those who followed the Lord alone, he was considered a pagan and most likely held to a religious syncretism or combining of religions. Bottom line: from Israel's perspective, God worked good through an unbeliever. The government was less than ideal, but at the end of the day, good flowed from it.

In the New Testament, this pattern of God working good regardless of the purity or lack thereof within the government is documented: Jesus stood before the Roman governor Pilate (John 18:28–19:16). During Pilate's interrogation, he said to Jesus, "You will not speak to me? Do You not know that I have authority to release You and authority to crucify You?" (John 19:10). Jesus answered him, "You would have no authority over Me at all unless it had been given you from above" (John 19:11).

The spine-chilling fact is that for all intents and purposes, the Lord told Pilate, "I have given you the power to crucify Me." God was in complete control, but to the world, it didn't seem that way. To the world, Jesus was being defeated through Pilate's sentence for Him to be crucified. Nevertheless, the greater reality was that through this counterintuitive verdict, the Lord would pay for the sins of the world. It seemed as if the government was losing its mind in the way the innocent Son of God was treated, but God's will was still being done (cf. Matthew 26:39; Mark 14:36; Luke 22:42).

Nevertheless, this overview of the believer's experience on the horizontal plane only confirms difficulty (at the very least). And this lack of horizontal peace is a humbling reality. Let's face it: we don't like it. How and why does this manifest in our country (besides the more obvious answers coming from Scripture and sacred theology)?

The Deterioration of Faith and Morality

Alexis de Tocqueville in discussing the political tensions inherent in early America—and certainly tensions that still exist—pointed out, "Do you not see that the religions are becoming weaker and that the divine notion of rights is disappearing? Do you not see that morals are being corrupted and that with them the moral notion of rights is fading?"[114] He was right. Today, there is perhaps no greater concern among Christians in America than the deterioration of the freedom of religion.

There is a reason for this, and this is no news flash (though perhaps we underestimate the issue): America is becoming increasingly secularized (a condition that jettisons God for the immediate and transitory gratifications of the culture), "and once a majority has formed on a question, there are virtually no obstacles which can, never mind stop, but even slow down its march and allow it the time to listen to the complaints of those it crushes in passing."[115]

As time advances, the march toward increased secularism keeps lockstep. Robert Bork saw this in connection to an important sociological principle:

> The "Durkheim constant." Emile Durkheim, a founder of sociology, posited that there is a limit to the amount of deviant behavior any community can "afford to recognize." As behavior worsens, the community adjusts its standards so that conduct once thought reprehensible is no longer deemed so.[116]

The Problem Identified: From Three to One Estates

I felt fortunate to be able to sit down with Dr. Russell Dawn (DPhil, Oxford University; JD, University of Colorado), president of Concordia University Chicago, to gain some clarity about this disturbing trend.[117] In any worthwhile analysis, the first step is to ensure the clarity of definitions. Dr. Dawn began with a crucial understanding of *politics*. It's interesting that general definitions of the word and concept relate

---

[114] Alexis de Tocqueville, *Democracy in America*, abr. Sanford Kessler, trans. Stephen D. Grant (Indianapolis: Hackett, 2000), 95.

[115] De Tocqueville, *Democracy in America*, 104.

[116] Robert H. Bork, *Slouching towards Gomorrah: Modern Liberalism and American Decline* (New York: HarperCollins, 1996), 3.

[117] Russell Dawn, interview by author, Irvine, California, January 15, 2020.

to the activities and human interactions with the governance of a country, but here the term *governance*—unfortunately in contemporary parlance—is reduced to the *state*. Refreshingly, however, Dr. Dawn took me back to a fuller meaning.

Politics for Dr. Dawn consists of human interactions within *three* estates, not only *one*. For him, any proper analysis of how the church needs to understand politics is that we live within three basic social units as intended by God: the church, the family, and the state. Dr. Dawn wasn't being novel. Luther wrote, "But the holy orders and true religious institutions established by God are these three: the office of priest, the estate of marriage, the civil government."[118] It goes without saying that Scripture is replete with this complete reality. (Luke 10:16 brings out our need to listen to the preaching office. Ephesians 4–5 and Colossians 3 are great examples about order in the family, and the Scriptures mentioned above—like Romans 13:1–7—cover the state.)

Having stated this full-orbed concept about what *politics* ought to always consider, Dr. Dawn was quick to diagnose the problem faced in our culture: "America's fundamental problem is that we have lost sight of the first two [estates]. As a result, there are those who want to make the state the entire realm and those who resist this as the state encroaches upon family and church. The battle, you see, is over the role of the state, meaning that politics becomes all about the third estate after all."

America, in other words—on both sides of the aisle—puts the third estate at the center of everyone's thoughts. In this way, we are suffering from a myopic view of society. As a result, people are not properly served because of neglect of the first two estates of church and family. This represents a void in our society's heart, and when people feel voids, they will try to fill them with whatever they can, which isn't always good.

The Results of Compromise

So, I asked Dr. Dawn, "How do we try to fill the void?" He was quick on the draw: "With emotions and passions, I believe . . . a lot of alarmism. [We have a] cancel culture going on. . . . If so and so thinks this wrong

---

[118] AE 37:164.

thing or says that wrong thing, or is involved in an evil institution, then these people are now canceled; we cannot accept anything about them." As bad a situation as this is, it doesn't end there. Dr. Dawn continued the thought line of the phenomena of a cancel culture: "We are sullied and tainted by this, so we can't even speak it, and it is this mentality that leads to the exaltation of passions so that whatever we hate, we hate everything that relates to it."

I had a feeling I knew where Dr. Dawn was going with this, but I formed the question anyway: "And where does the Christian faith fit into this?" His answer was bold and hard to hear, but rang true: "Christianity is becoming taboo . . . in fact, Christianity is the ultimate taboo . . . because the Gospel implies the Law and this tells us that we are not okay, and if there is anything we have to be, then it is that we must be okay. If what drives us is anything but good, then it is unacceptable. Christianity is the ultimate thing our culture is trying to get rid of. The secularists have immanentized the eschaton, that is, turned the Christian hope of heavenly bliss into a humanist hope of earthly bliss. That earthly bliss can only be attained by destruction, by getting rid of the people who hold taboo ideas. Ultimately, that means getting rid of Christians."

How has it come to this? Bork observes, "It was tempting for men who wanted freedom from religious prohibitions to accept the idea [of] . . . steadily disproving religion's claims."[119] He goes on to cite three main examples contributing to the cultural metamorphosis:

1. Sigmund Freud categorized religion as illusion and recast it as a form of neurosis.

2. Karl Marx viewed religion as superstition that opposed the working class.

3. Charles Darwin offered evolution, removing the need for a Creator.[120]

---

[119] Bork, *Slouching towards Gomorrah*, 281.

[120] Bork, *Slouching towards Gomorrah*, 281.

Bork sees the result that, because the new forces that drive life are characteristically immoral, "inhibitions are not only passé but dangerous."[121] Since Christianity represents inhibitions (recall Dr. Dawn's insight that Gospel implies Law), then Christianity is considered dangerous, and what is considered dangerous must be snuffed out. Another surveyor of culture sees this: "History thus dechristianized has no moral limitations. 'Right' is a moving target, propelled by the march of facts and sentiments."[122] So, what is the Church doing about this? Schlossberg is convicting if not damning:

> Meanwhile, we are left with a church that to a large extent has chosen to befriend the powers that dominate the world instead of judging them. We should be reminded that the crucifixion of Christ was a joint production, instigated by religious authorities and then carried out by the state. When the state joins forces with [cultural idols] in forging the great brutalities of the future, we should not be surprised to find the representatives of the establishment churches, fuglemen for the idolatries, earnestly assuring us that God's will is being done.[123]

Schlossberg sounds like de Tocqueville: "Those who had at first rejected it as false end up accepting it as general, and those who continue to oppose it in the depths of their hearts show nothing of what they feel; they take good care not to engage in a dangerous and useless struggle."[124]

Engagement Triangle Point 2: People and Attitude

Do Not Fear, Little Flock

The situation on the national level permeating American culture leaves little room for the Christian to feel anything but overwhelmed. All this amounts to what feels like a cultural tsunami. Where do we even

---

[121] Bork, *Slouching towards Gomorrah*, 281.

[122] Herbert Schlossberg, *Idols for Destruction: The Confict of Christian Faith and American Culture* (Wheaton, IL: Crossway Books, 1993), 37.

[123] Schlossberg, *Idols for Destruction*, 259.

[124] Tocqueville, *Democracy in America*, 295.

begin to face this? The Christian Church should be lifted by these words of the Lord Jesus Christ: "Fear not, little flock, for it is your Father's good pleasure to give you the kingdom" (Luke 12:32). The context here is regarding anxiety where our Lord taught, "Therefore I tell you, do not be anxious about your life" (Luke 12:22). The Lord promises to cover all our necessities as God's grace provides for both body and soul. Nothing can change this for the child of God. This does not, however, also mean that we enter a life of quietism. The Lord taught that Christians are also the salt of the earth (Matthew 5:13), a metaphor that points to a preserving usefulness for the world that God works through His people. At the same time, this does not mean that we go to the opposite end of things, to an extreme activism that loses sight of the bigger picture (remember *the kingdom* already belongs to those in Christ).

Engaging Whoever Is in Your Path

I was inspired by the way Dr. Dawn put it when I asked him, "How can a Christian make things better?" With wisdom, he replied, "Don't try to go out to change the world, but instead go serve, serve your family, serve your boss, serve your client, serve whoever is in your path." This was the counsel I needed for launching that aspect of engagement for the Gospel that bridges with one person at a time.

PEOPLE

● ATTITUDE
- All People Desire
  Freedom & Peace

When it comes to engagement with people with strong political views, however, what is the best way to bridge, and how do we even begin to establish common ground? I needed to access someone who not only had a grasp of politics, but also an understanding of the people interacting with it. Dr. Paul Fick (PhD in clinical psychology from what is now Alliant International University) is not only a gifted therapist but has proven himself to be a keen political observer. He authored the book *The Dysfunctional President* (1995, 1996, 1998), which provided the definitive psychological analysis of Bill Clinton. *The New York Post* hailed the book to be "prophetic," since Dr. Fick predicted in 1995 that Clinton would act out sexually during his administration in a manner that would risk his presidency. He has been the guest for well over one hundred television and radio interviews. He offers an insightful vantage point for American political insight, especially since our consideration here is not simply politics per se, but *how politics impacts human engagement so that people would know God's love.*[125]

To begin with, I realized immediately that Dr. Fick is lucid regarding the political-cultural malady we outlined above. I asked, "Dr. Fick, how do you see the political divide in our nation?" He was thoughtful but unhesitant: "I think that the increasing divide we see in the political arena is predicated on the division between the concept of America [as having rights from God to government] and those that have a vision of America that is quite different than that. . . . There is an increasing movement to eliminate the influence of Christianity within our government and across the societal spectrum."

He elaborated, "[And this] impacts the way we live as a society; it influences culture and affects every part of our lives, especially our religious liberty. For the sake of religious liberty alone, we should treat it seriously and be active in our citizenship. Keep in mind that many political leaders are, in fact, devout Christians." I was sold that we indeed have much at stake, but how does the Christian begin to engage someone passionate about politics?

Humble Hearts That Listen to People

Dr. Fick emphasized humility: "When we engage people, it is important to avoid giving the impression that we know where they're coming from. *We don't.* Don't make assumptions. *People are motivated to have their*

---

[125] Paul Fick, interview by author, Laguna Niguel, California, December 26, 2019, and January 28, 2020.

position for a variety of reasons." I asked for examples and realized that Dr. Fick didn't simply mean there are different motives for political views among people, but that *individual persons have within themselves multiple reasons for their position.* Dr. Fick explained, "People form their politics from a wide variety of sources; worldviews have multiple contributors, and form what is referred to in psychology as a *schema* and forms how a person views the world and life. We have to understand that the person in front of you has gathered elements for their position from parents, their experience, personal crises, philosophical underpinnings, et cetera [and that therefore] the Christian cannot assume that that person shares their Christian worldview."

So, in simple terms, he recommended, "We must be good listeners. It's important, therefore, to listen first. Make sure you understand their position to the best of your ability. Then repeat it back to them. Don't give them the impression that you agree with them when you don't, but demonstrate respect and willingness to listen. Then ask if they are willing to listen to you."

Dr. Fick was providing a detailed description of **engagement**. We are equipped with a biblical **perspective** understanding the divisiveness (and it is of no surprise to us; the Lord teaches us exactly what to expect). But as we are now engaging with **people**, the Christian is not trying to deepen the divide, but in leaving hostility and defensiveness to the wind, seeks to express genuine humility. The goal now is to listen and put on the shoes of the one for whom Christ loves as much as He loves the engaged Christian.

As Dr. Fick was describing how the Christian should always conduct themselves, he was at the same time leading all Christians to conduct a serious gut check going into any political engagement with someone with opposing views: "Check your own motivation. It can't be about trying to win an argument."

Since he mentioned the word *argument*—with the important detail that it is one thing to argue, but another to be *argumentative*, something the Christian should always avoid—he reminded me of what Dr. Dawn said about the culture resultantly being led to engage with emotions, passion, and alarmism. Of course, I wanted to hear Dr. Fick's take on why things can get extreme in a heartbeat.

Many Motives behind Political Views

He was ready for the question: "For some, politics is in their lifeblood, and [they] are fueled by despair and anger. Ultimately, anytime you place the temporal, including your political viewpoint, on too high of a pedestal, you are begging for trouble." I was fascinated by this. Why would anyone take politics this far?

Dr. Fick explained what he qualified to be a very general insight about situations when passion over politics is in the extreme. These motivations might indicate that other issues are involved:

1. About one-third of people desire to be lovable and good, so their politics is an expression of doing good for others.

2. About one-third desire to be in control and not wrong, so their politics is for being hungry for power.

3. About one-third desire self-worth and value, so their politics is for validation.

And none of these are for the Christian to judge their neighbor. What Dr. Fick was really setting the table for is the priority of compassion during engagement: "When someone 'over-attaches' to something— especially a cause, in this case, politics—it is usually because they sense a lack of worth or value in themselves. By connecting with a cause . . . the person formulates a veneer or purpose in his or her life, but politics is ever-changing and entire platforms and systems can be lost. We can't base our lives on this."

Common Ground

Dr. Dawn reinforced much of what Dr. Fick was outlining. Dr. Dawn pointed out that Christians should be "politically humble enough to establish common ground." He reminded me that there is far more that unites us than divides us. "What do we all have in common?" Dr. Dawn answered his own question, "Our desire for freedom, respect, peace . . . in many ways, we desire the same personal outcomes; not necessarily societal outcomes, but respect, freedom, and peace for ourselves . . . security. Anger comes especially regarding *the how*, not so much the end."

When we dig enough—asking questions, checking assumptions, thoroughly respecting and understanding—we can easily discover that at the end of the day, as Dr. Dawn was quick to point out: "What people are missing from an existential standpoint is a sure and certain hope. Deep inside us, most of us know . . . that we are not what we say we are. We are not thoroughly good, and our hopes for an earthly paradise are doomed for failure."

And this is where engagement for Christ becomes inestimably valuable: the Gospel gives hope that can't be lost. Dr. Dawn put it simply, "My only hope is in Christ, who forgives me for how I fall short."

Engagement Triangle Point 3: Place and Cultural Influence

When Politics Defines a Person

Recall in chapter 3 regarding the thorough understanding of **place** that there are invisible influences behind the culture we see with our eyes. The Christian knows that principalities and powers (Ephesians 6:12) are real, and they impact the world we interact with. Keller asks a vital question to remind Christians of what is really going on when political hostilities rule the day:

> How does this destruction of social relationships flow from the internal effects of sin? If we get our very identity, our sense of worth, from our political position, then politics isn't really about politics, but about *us*. Through our cause we are getting a self, our worth. That means we *must* demonize the opposition.[126]

---

[126]   Keller, *Reason for God*, 175.

PLACE

● CULTURE
- Resist Being Militant or Silent

Christians can't join this bandwagon. When we can rather show the one with whom we are engaging that we are willing to hear and respect them; when we can be self-deprecating since no politician or platform we might support is without fault; when we can be willing to grant whatever is positive in the other's view; and when we can remind ourselves what we have in common, then this may be the moment in time for the Gospel to be shared. This is when the powers of the world that attempt to fill people with hatred will have to succumb to the One whose blood covers all hatred, showing the truth that "love covers a multitude of sins" (1 Peter 4:8).

The Temptation to Become Militant

Politics in America wants to control the way Christians think, to make the Christian believe that God attaches Himself to one political party. God, however, is immutable and will not be defined by fluctuating platforms. He is also steadfast and will not conform to parties, which invariably compromise their own positions. To forget these things, and yet insist that God is on *our side* while accusing the other side of inherent evil, forgets what Jesus taught: "You hypocrite, first take the log out of your own eye, and then you will see clearly to take the speck out of your brother's eye" (Matthew 7:5). To forget this is to permit a militancy that shows nothing of the priority of the Gospel.

The Temptation to Become Silent

The worldly influence doesn't stop there, however, and would also tempt the Christian to go the other way: to not say anything at all. I've elaborated elsewhere:

> The great irony of those trying to limit the Christian voice in the public square is that they, too, have a religious world-view when "religion" includes any position about God. When Christians debate atheists about these matters, it is not that one side is religious and the other is not. Rather, both parties hold to theological viewpoints. One says that God exists, and the other says God does not exist. Both belief systems about God easily influence what follows in their respective ethics and morality. These, in turn, further impact the culture for all people.[127]

Hauerwas and Willimon have observed: "*Everyone* is, in some way or another, a subject of conversion. All knowing, including the notion that 'religion is a very private matter between me and God,' is externally, socially derived."[128] This idea is not only foreign to the faith but even to the First Amendment of the US Constitution. Any argument with respect to the separation of church and state ought not be confused with a separation of religion and politics. The impetus for the concept of separation was not to silence the church but to ensure that no singular sect would dominate representation in the state.

The Balance for the Gospel

So, what is the Christian's response to cultural influence? The answer is the middle road: not activism that would misrepresent the Christ, who desires that His people remain cognizant of a greater kingdom; nor quietism that would stand idly by in the face of attempts to remove religious freedom. That is, the Christian always loves his or her neighbor, and always honors God. *This* is the balance.

---

[127] Espinosa, *Faith That Sees through the Culture*, 162.

[128] Hauerwas and Willimon, *Where Resident Aliens Live*, 81.

In the meantime, Christians make the most of opportunities to engage by equipping themselves as much as possible. Dr. Dawn reminds Christians: "Don't just blurt something out. For example, know *why* God has created marriage as He did. . . . The world wants reasons . . . there are *reasons* for what Scripture says, so educate yourself. . . . If marriage is just for happiness and fulfillment of the two people wanting to marry, [then the cultural-political movements devoid of God are correct]." There must be more. The Word of Christ offers more.

Along the way, what will guard the Church's mission to engage is to remember that it is not as if the Christian is getting into the boat to engage someone without the Gospel, but rather to know that Christians are *already* in that same boat.[129] Christians always engage fellow sinners who need the love and mercy of God, who need the hope that human politics cannot in the end provide. So, in humility, we who are in Christ do not "think that the world is more evil than we, that we are redeemed and the world is fallen. We believe [instead] that the world and the church are both fallen *and* redeemed by the cross of Christ."[130]

---

[129] One of my gifted parishioners who wished to remain anonymous improved my statement that Christians get into the same boat as unbelievers. His version is better: Christians *already are*!

[130] Hauerwas and Willimon, *Where Resident Aliens Live*, 53.

CHAPTER **8** DISCUSSION GUIDE

ENGAGING POLITICS

UNCOVER INFORMATION

1. Why does Christian faith say that the state (government) is good (in spite of its many shortcomings)?

2. Where did Pontius Pilate's authority to crucify Jesus come from?

3. List the three estates that form the left-hand kingdom and proper governance.

4. What did Freud, Marx, and Darwin put forth?

5. Dr. Dawn reminds us *what* about common ground?

DISCOVER MEANING

1. Why do Hauerwas and Willimon refer to Christians as *resident aliens*?

2. By permitting Pilate to condemn Him, what was Jesus accomplishing through a political situation that was a miscarriage of governmental justice?

3. Why are all three estates needed?

4. Why did Dr. Dawn say that Christianity is becoming taboo? What did he mean?

5. To help us be compassionate, Dr. Fick explains three basic motivations that might be behind the political positions we encounter. What does this mean for considerate engagement?

EXPLORE IMPLICATIONS

1. God called the Persian King Cyrus His "shepherd" and "anointed," but Cyrus was not a true believer in the Lord. Still, God worked through him to bless Israel. How might we apply this lesson to our own situation?

2. If Alexis de Tocqueville was right about religion becoming weaker in our nation and if the "Durkheim constant" is also true, then what should we expect from our culture?

3. If the three estates are reduced to one (which is what is occurring), what problems result?

4. If Christianity stands for inhibitions against immorality, how will the culture respond?

5. How is engagement for the Gospel negatively impacted if Christians are militant? if they are quiet?

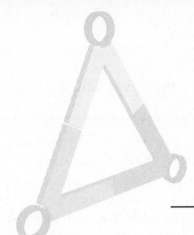

CHAPTER 9:
ENGAGING PERSONHOOD

Small Catechism

The Fifth Commandment: You shall not murder.

What does this mean? We should fear and love God so that we do not hurt or harm our neighbor in his body, but help and support him in every physical need.

Large Catechism

The Fifth Commandment: It also applies to anyone who can do his neighbor good, prevent or resist evil, defend, and save his neighbor so that no bodily harm or hurt happen to him—yet does not do this [James 2:15–16]. . . . Therefore, it is God's ultimate purpose that we let harm come to no one, but show him all good and love.[131]

Engagement Triangle Point 1: Perspective and Approach

What is a *Person*?

In the first two chapters of Holy Scripture, the picture of personhood comes into focus. Moses recorded at Genesis 1:26–27: "Then God

---

[131] LC I 189, 193.

said, 'Let Us make man in Our image, after Our likeness. . . . So God created man in His own image, in the image of God He created him; male and female He created them." In addition, we have been given Genesis 2:7: "Then the LORD God formed the man of dust from the ground and breathed into his nostrils the breath of life, and the man became a living creature." From these, Scripture teaches that a person is both body from the earth and *breath* (the Hebrew for *soul* or *spirit*) from God, but not *any* body and soul, but one first made in the very image and likeness of God in the *narrow sense* of original righteousness.

While this loss of the original image means that sin and death have taken over humanity, God has nevertheless treated every person with body and soul with a sanctity demonstrated by the fact that they are persons for whom the Son of God, Jesus Christ, came to be among, live for, die for, rise for, ascend and reign for. Furthermore, the emphasis of Jesus for the *world* cannot be overemphasized, as it guarantees the salvation Jesus purchased is for every *person* so that it may be personally acquired when any person through faith holds to Christ.

PERSPECTIVE

● APPROACH
- Defend Sanctity
  of All Persons

So, what makes a person a person? A person is specially created by God to have both body and soul, a soul having come directly from God so that—originally—the person was in the image of God in the narrow sense. What is more, for the sake of restoring this former image, God has sent His Son in holy love for every person to the extent that this divine love grants sanctity for every person for whom Jesus shed His atoning blood. In short, *a person is one distinctive individual with a body and a soul especially loved by God and is thus sacred to God.* No single person falls out of this definition of personhood.

Our culture is so prone, however, to look for exceptions to the rule. God's Word, however, is open and shut on this: "every person" means *every single one*. Everyone who falls under the category of a distinct individual having body and soul originally from the breath of God is, therefore, one for whom Jesus won salvation—a **person**.

The Unborn and Infants: Full Persons

"Ah, but there *is* an exception: the unborn!" No, they are *not* exceptions, and for this reason alone, abortion commits murder, because the unborn are also *persons*. Not only has science confirmed the distinct personhood of the unborn in relation to their mothers, but the Scriptures indicate God's immediate and caring relationship to all *persons* in the womb:

> For [God] formed my inward parts; You knitted me together in my mother's womb. I praise You, for I am fearfully and wonderfully made. Wonderful are Your works; my soul knows it very well. My frame was not hidden from You, when I was being made in secret, intricately woven in the depths of the earth. Your eyes saw my unformed substance; in Your book were written, every one of them, the days that were formed for me, when as yet there was none of them. (Psalm 139:13–16)

For those who are not yet born or newly born, the Holy Scriptures herald their sanctity. One unique meeting between two extremely small persons in Holy Scripture is most famous. The first time Jesus Christ came up to His cousin John the Baptist, John was so overjoyed—he couldn't help himself—he had to *leap*! When did this meeting between these two holy persons occur? Luke 1:39–44 records that it happened when both Jesus and John were still in their respective mother's *womb*: John inside Elizabeth and the Christ inside Mary. When Elizabeth and Mary were face-to-face, John knew Jesus was close to him, and he couldn't hold back his joy *while still in the womb*!

To punctuate this status of the very young, the Holy Scriptures will not permit the Sacrament of initiation (Holy Baptism) into the

Church to bypass little ones. This is what we know that demonstrates the dignity of the full personhood of little ones:

1. They need Holy Baptism on account of their inherited sin (Psalm 51:5), so God has provided a Means of Grace for them since God sent Christ for the *world*.

2. They are included for Holy Baptism on account of Christ's commission to baptize all *nations* (all people from all places, Matthew 28:19); on account of the household Baptisms in the Book of Acts, where *households* might include infants (e.g., Acts 16:33); on account of the comparison of Israel having been baptized into Moses (1 Corinthians 10:2), which beyond question included the very young; and on account that Baptism is presented as the new *circumcision of Christ*, recalling when Old Testament circumcision was applied: the little one was only *eight days old* (Genesis 17:12).

3. They are capable of faith for receiving Holy Baptism (Psalm 22:9). Christ the Lord referenced Psalm 8:2 when He said, "Out of the mouth of infants and nursing babies You have prepared praise" (Matthew 21:16). The translation "nursing babies" is spot-on and epitomizes a helpless *suckling*, and *such a one when granted faith by the Holy Spirit praises God*!

God has declared the unborn and newly born to be full persons: known personally by Him in the womb, given the gift of full lives already seen by God, identified as those with body and soul, and capable of receiving the gift of faith while in the womb (consider John who leaped, Luke 1:41, 44) or as infants who are therefore candidates for the sacred Sacrament of Holy Baptism. This is called treating the unborn or recently born in *sanctity*, *as sacred*, and *as holy*.

To treat these in this way is to simultaneously honor God as holy, who reveals the sanctity of little ones. But to go the other way is not simply depriving babies of *their* sanctity but denies God of *His* sanctity. Our culture, however, has taken this assault and run with it. There are of course reasons for this. In a word, the problem is *secularism*.[132] Let's examine a case study of what this looks like.

Secularism

Dr. Yuval Noah Harari (PhD from Oxford, historian, philosopher, and best-selling author) offers one of the clearest articulations against the faith, which—as we will show—invariably leads to the results of secularism, including the devaluation of *person*. With an understanding of his perspective, however, we gain valuable insight for potential engagement not only for reaching people like Dr. Harari, who is also loved by Jesus Christ as much as anyone, but also for defending those who cannot defend themselves from the ramifications of his teaching.

First in his view, the sacred texts of religions are irreparably undermined since they are constantly *reinterpreted* by their own religious scholars.[133] He does not hesitate, of course, to include the Christian faith in this evaluation. Second in his argument, the religions have formed *mass identities*, but these "*are based on fictional stories*."[134] Harari explains, "Religions, rites, and rituals will remain important as long as the power of humankind rests on mass cooperation and as long as mass cooperation rests on belief in shared fictions."[135] His conclusion has vast implications:

> To the best of our scientific understanding, none of the thousands of stories that different cultures, religions, and tribes have invented throughout history is true. They are all just human inventions. If you ask for the true meaning of life and get a story in reply, know that this is the wrong answer. The exact details don't really matter. *Any* story is wrong, simply for being a story. The universe just does not work like a story.[136]

---

[132] Something we referred to as *secular age* in chapter 7, and *secularized* culture in chapter 8.

[133] Yuval Noah Harari, *21 Lessons for the 21st Century*, Spiegel & Grau Trade Paperback Edition (New York: Spiegel & Grau, 2019), 134.

[134] Harari, *21 Lessons*, 137.

[135] Harari, *21 Lessons*, 141.

[136] Harari, *21 Lessons*, 287.

Christian Apologetic

Three things must be dealt with immediately:

1. His assumption that the existence of reinterpretation implies no *correct* interpretation that effectively renders the Scriptures— assumed to be based on "fictional stories" and "shared fictions"—unreliable.

2. His inference that science supports his position.

3. His conclusion that *any* story that answers the true meaning of life is out of necessity untrue *precisely because it is a story*.

Let's start with the last point and work backward. First, in my discussions with my doctoral mentor at the University of Birmingham, England, I became better acquainted with the use of the word *story*.[137] If nothing else happens when Americans study in England, a better grasp of English normally ensues. It is fallacious to always take *story* as a fictional account. *Story* etymologically refers to *history*, and history is full of true and factual accounting. These accounts about real people in real places in real history are also *stories*.

Harari, however, wants to have his cake and eat it too. He wants to imply that the story from the Christian faith is a *fictional* story, while *his* story is rock-solid *non-fiction*. At the same time, he doesn't specify between *stories*, so he paints himself into a corner: "If you ask for the true meaning of life and get a story in reply, know that this is the wrong answer. The exact details don't really matter. *Any* story is wrong, simply for being a story." With his own specified criterion, we can't believe *his* story—his accounting of the universe and life—to be accurate either.

Second, Harari—not speaking as a scientist—commits exactly what we warned about in chapter 7: he takes "science" beyond its purview. Alister McGrath, who *is* a scientist (PhD from Oxford in molecular biophysics) as well as a theologian, helps us retain boundaries: "Nature

---

[137] While Dr. Marius Felderhof and I had different theological positions, he taught me the next level for research and writing, something I will forever be grateful for.

is not studied with any expectation that it will offer a 'proof' of the existence of God."[138] Timothy Keller backs McGrath: "Because science's baseline methodology is to always assume a natural cause for every phenomenon, there is no experiment that could prove *or* disprove that there is something beyond this material world."[139]

In spite of this, Harari implies because "the best of our scientific understanding" cannot verify the stories of religion, that this means—somehow—that science is on the side of *his* worldview. This is misleading at best.

Lastly, he commits a glaring non sequitur by asserting that because the Scriptures have been *reinterpreted* that therefore *the correct interpretation* either doesn't exist or if it did, it would not reveal what is real and true. At this point, we arrive at a popular move to discredit the faith: if there is a known example or examples of a miscarriage of what the faith confesses, then it must follow that the faith itself is unreliable. Harari doesn't hold back: "Christianity has been responsible for great crimes such as the Inquisition, the Crusades, the oppression of native cultures across the world, and the disempowerment of women."[140] *So, if you find a wrong act within a system, then the whole system is wrong.*

Nobody consistently holds this standard in real life. No one would say that because this error in engineering led to the death of x number of people, or that misapplication of science led to the demise of y number of people, *therefore, engineering and science are illegitimate disciplines.* In the same way, just because the Scriptures *have* been reinterpreted or misinterpreted, that doesn't mean the Scriptures *themselves* cannot be rightly interpreted to reveal what is real and true. Moreover, because some who profess Christ are guilty of having committed horrific acts, this does not mean that these reflected the *right* teaching and practice of the Christian faith. At least Harari gives us a better sense of what he relies upon.

---

138 McGrath, *Fine-Tuned Universe*, 34.

139 Keller, *Making Sense of God*, 35.

140 Harari, *21 Lessons*, 219.

How Secularism Impacts Culture and Personhood

Why consider these things with respect to *what is a person*? Because if the legitimacy and truth of the Holy Scriptures are rejected, and its teaching is reduced to "fictional stories" and "shared fictions," *then God who reveals the sanctity of persons is removed from human culture, and the definition of* **person** *and the value of* **persons** *is up for grabs.*

In rejecting the authority of God's Word, secularism has exchanged God's sanctity of personhood for valuing people only to the extent that they are considered useful. With God's Word and God Himself relegated to irrelevance, secularism promotes humanity as "the norm of all knowledge of truth, value, and being."[141] This is *exactly* what Harari asserts: "Secularism can provide us with all the values we need."[142] Still, are we making an invalid assumption that secularism is incapable of properly protecting and honoring personhood? Let's consider the basis for our concern.

Since secularism removes God's Word, God's Law is also removed. If God's Law is removed, then right and wrong beyond relativism are removed. Schlossberg sees what has happened: "Nobody who rejects the . . . commandments' call to reject idols and [not reject] worship [of] the true and living God can be expected to recognize any ultimate significance in the . . . commandments' ethical requirements."[143] In other words, to reject God is to reject the treatment of persons. If God is no longer recognized, then some people will no longer be valued or treated as fully human. But does our argument invest too much in the necessity of God's Law?

Our culture is already recognizably in a tailspin while promoting secularism and *demonstrates that it generates lawlessness.* There is no question now as to who is in charge: "Here is a simple but profound rule: *If there are no absolutes by which to judge society, then society is absolute.*"[144] As Francis Schaeffer points out, this will lead to the loss

---

[141] Sproul, Gerstner, and Lindsley, *Classical Apologetics*, 8.

[142] Harari, *21 Lessons*, 208.

[143] Schlossberg, *Idols for Destruction*, 47.

[144] Francis A. Schaeffer, *How Should We Then Live? The Rise and Decline of Western Thought and Culture*, Crossway Books Paperback (Westchester, IL: Crossway Books, 1983), 224.

of meaning and values since the society is transitory and unstable. The result includes degeneracy, decadence, depravity, and a love of violence for violence's sake.[145] Schaeffer borrows from Edward Gibbon five attributes that marked Rome's end as analyzed in *Decline and Fall of the Roman Empire*:

1. A mounting love of show and luxury (affluence).

2. A widening gap between the rich and the poor.

3. An obsession with sex.

4. A freakishness in the arts and enthusiasm pretending to be creativity.

5. An increased desire to live off the state.[146]

Within such a cultural milieu, "killing is an action, like any other, that must be judged on pragmatic grounds."[147] And here is the terrifying part that logically follows: "The arguments in favor of abortion, infanticide, and euthanasia reveal that the humanitarian ethic wishes to restrict the right to live and expand the right to die—and to kill."[148]

So, what of the *person*? *If they are weak, unable to defend themselves, considered undesirable or detestable, these persons will no longer be treated as persons to the extent that the culture will turn its back on them.* Jesus warned as He spoke of the end times: "And because lawlessness will be increased, the love of many will grow cold" (Matthew 24:12). The Church has been given its marching orders, however, for those considered persons, *and it begins with a robust commitment to engage for the sake of those the world wants to forget.*

The Christian Faith Upholds Personhood

No worldview upholds the sanctity of all *persons* as does the Christian faith. In addition to all that has already been said regarding little ones,

---

[145] Schaeffer, *How Should We Then Live?*, 226.

[146] Schaeffer, *How Should We Then Live?*, 227.

[147] Schlossberg, *Idols for Destruction*, 78.

[148] Schlossberg, *Idols for Destruction*, 82.

Christ taught in Matthew 25:35–36 that the Church is called to serve the hungry and thirsty, strangers without shelter, those needing clothing, and those sick and in prison. Christ demonstrated that the outcast are not outcast to God (as He healed the leper in Matthew 8:2–3), and what is probably glossed over too much is that Jesus served the demon-possessed, who would have been repulsive to other people (Matthew 8:16). Proverbs 31:8–9 directs Christians: "Open your mouth for the mute, for the rights of all who are destitute. Open your mouth, judge righteously, defend the rights of the poor and needy." And the Lord commands, "You shall stand up before the gray head and honor the face of an old man" (Leviticus 19:32). James condemns relegating the poor so that Christians acknowledge the admonition, "Have you not then made distinctions among yourselves and become judges with evil thoughts?" (James 2:4). If there was ever a time to engage for the sake of the Gospel and for the sake of those denied their full personhood, the time is now. The unborn, the newly born, those with special needs, those who are broken, those who are sick, and those who are elderly: these are the ones we treat as fully human and engage in the name of Jesus.

Engagement Triangle Point 2: People and Attitude

Engaging People with Special Needs

Dr. Cari Chittick, EdD, educational leadership in higher education, is a professor at Concordia University, Irvine who specializes in special education. I felt fortunate for her contribution as it was evident that she is not only impeccable in her field but also someone who emanates the love of Christ. If anyone fights against the cultural trends to treat those with special needs—or those who learn differently—as less than full persons, then it is Dr. Chittick. They, too, should be engaged for the sake of sharing the Gospel. She has devoted her life to this. I was eager to dive into this interview.[149]

Dr. Chittick was inspired to enter her field by those she grew up around. A grandmother had developed polio at thirty-three years of age, and through tremendous physical difficulties—from braces on

---

[149] Cari Chittick, interview by author, Lake Forest, California, December 13, 2019.

her legs and the use of crutches, to being confined to a wheelchair—continued to serve her family, especially her boys, to ensure they knew she loved them. Dr. Chittick also witnessed the trials of a neighbor of her great-grandmother with Down syndrome and a gentleman in her church with significant vision impairment. She witnessed at an early age that those who deal with these things are people. She was also moved by how her grandmother and grandfather partnered through hard times, making it work through their love for each other. Dr. Chittick summarized what it did for her: "My lens was not typical, but it helped pave my vocational path, and it helped me to have a heart of love and compassion."

PEOPLE

● **ATTITUDE**
- Look past Problem
  & See the Person

Because we are tempted by the culture to not think about those with special needs, Christians can struggle to imagine how to engage, but first I wanted to know why it was even an issue. "Dr. Chittick, why do you think we struggle and are intimidated toward engaging people with special needs?" Dr. Chittick wasn't a stranger to understanding the problem: "In layman's terms, it's because of ignorance, because people are generally afraid of what they don't know. Often, our expectations may be different . . . there's a fear . . . and this boils down to ignorance."

That made sense to me, so the next question was easy to formulate: "What can we do about this?" Dr. Chittick encourages Christians to delve right into building a relationship with a person who has special needs: "You get to know people by engaging [didn't this sound familiar!], say hello, communicate. People with special needs have a different spectrum of communication skills. As a society though, we judge. Society says, 'You have to look like this; you have to be this way,' but everyone is beautiful. Someone with autism, for instance, will have gifts that surpass others." I was intrigued by her choice of words, especially *gifts*.

Gifted Ones

I didn't so much ask a question as make a statement: "It seems a little challenging if not counterintuitive that someone with special needs and who has had to struggle more would—as a result of a seeming disadvantage—be perceived as someone who is *gifted*." Dr. Chittick didn't want to mince words, "There is giftedness in having special needs. These are *truly* gifts. I'm not just saying that." This was a key juncture to the common ground that is needed to connect for the sake of engagement: When the Christian engages anyone, then it must be with the foregone conclusion and conviction that this person we engage with is gifted by God. Furthermore, what is meant by *gifted* is that they are given an exceptional status or ability that *can* help others and improve the community. Theological precision was not lost on me as I listened, and I reminded myself that there is a duality even within *giftedness*. Yes, those in Christ are also given the Holy Spirit, who works His gifts through the members of the Holy Church, *but it is also true that all exceptional skills and abilities bestowed on all people are also gifts from God*. Without this honor and respect going into engagement with someone with special needs, the engagement will fall flat.

I was learning and wanted to learn more: "Okay, Dr. Chittick, how do we go about actually engaging then?" Dr. Chittick's expertise was evident: "We need to accept that it takes time to get to know someone, so we have to be patient and *listen*. At the same time, we have to respect people by using people-first language."

Person-First Language

I needed clarification. "People-first language?" Dr. Chittick explained, "We use people-first language when we recognize that a person is a person *first*, who then happens to also use a wheelchair, have blue eyes, or deals with whatever thing they are dealing with. This means that we immediately give value to their personhood and *then* respect the component they live with. For example, instead of referring to 'an autistic person,' we should say 'a *person* with autism.' Using person-first language shows *respect*! Once upon a time, we separated people with special needs, but now we're more inclusive, hiring into the workforce. Instead of being hidden, there is inclusion. The Americans with Disabilities Act (ADA) was tremendously important for persons with disabilities as it created a societal shift of inclusion of all people into public life."

Dr. Chittick had impressed upon me a great feel for honoring and respecting a person with special needs, but I needed to get to the nitty-gritty for engaging for the Gospel. "Dr. Chittick, how do we engage with the goal of sharing the Gospel?" Dr. Chittick began with an image of Christ: "Christ is the teacher. We should emulate Him. He taught by asking questions. Approach with a smile, with a hug or a fist bump, and offer an invitation for conversation with the goal of building a foundation of trust and love. Picture yourself with a person with Down syndrome: You're respecting them, loving them . . . and then ask a question. As you do, don't judge or assume. They have a greater capacity than you think. Encourage them with the goal of *celebrating life*. Remind yourself that you are sharing the Gospel not only with your words but with your actions. When you start to feel a connection, say, 'Let me tell you about Jesus . . . even though I'm an awful, terrible person, I'm forgiven by my great God, who wants me to be with Him forever.' Step out of your comfort zone. . . . Let the Holy Spirit work through you. Show interest in their achievements."

Beautiful Ones

And then Dr. Chittick said something that truly captivated me: "There is brokenness in the world because of sin, but God makes broken beautiful." This was now the second time Dr. Chittick had referred to *beauty*, and it revealed a lot about her approach. Not only are those with special needs gifted, but even in their brokenness—as *all* people are broken—they are also beautiful. *This takes eyes of faith to see as God sees so that full personhood is affirmed and acknowledged.*

In this process, Dr. Chittick then took me to some important details for sharing the Gospel: "As you engage and ask questions, ask yourself, 'What's going to speak to this unique person?' For example, if the person loves food, find a connection between God's Word and food. If you're engaging with a person with autism, things are very literal, so use a very literal approach." Dr. Chittick was taking me back to 1 Corinthians 9:22: "I have become all things to all people, that by all means I might save some."

Don't Forget the Caregivers

I was pleasantly surprised when Dr. Chittick led me to another realm of consideration I hadn't thought of: What about the *caregivers* of those with special needs? Dr. Chittick reminded me that oftentimes, "They are tired, even exhausted; sometimes too tired to go to church. They might have some resentment. To engage them, we should invite them to birthday parties, to lunch, to coffee, or whatever activity, and not be afraid [to include them], and this is when we often find a lot of tears. . . . Too often people don't include and don't invite. Ask questions to the caregiver too, and remember not to assume anything. Remember that Jesus served the lepers, being open to embrace differences. When they share that they have resentment, feeling as though they've been dealt a bad hand, call your pastor [or remain engaged so that], somehow you get to a mental shift: *life is tough, but God is tougher* [than whatever life is throwing at you]. . . . Affirm their feelings, and say something like, 'Hey, yeah this is tough, but you are loved by God and have a community of faith [if indeed it is nearby].' Offer up an ear. A lot of times an ear—just listening and asking questions—makes a difference. Keyword: *invest!*"

I liked Dr. Chittick's keyword *invest*. It's an engagement word that reminds us that this is what Christ did for us: *He invested His entire life into us and considered all of us invaluable, each and every one of us a full person, loved by God.* Indeed, this one thing alone gives us vital common ground with any person we might speak to with special needs: we are invaluable to God and, as Dr. Chittick said, *gifted* and *beautiful.*

Engaging the Broken

I was being reminded as to why the second point of the engagement triangle—*person*—was so important: we must consider the unique person we engage with. My next interview represented a major shift and a new set of considerations. I was led to Dr. Kristen Koenig, who has a DPhil in sociology from the University of York, England, and is a professor of sociology at Concordia University, Irvine. I was about to be challenged and blessed at the same time.[150]

Once when I was helping lead a defending life conference, someone accused me and all other Christians of only focusing on the unborn and then forgetting about people after they're born. It was a terrible thing to hear. By God's grace, I have felt fortunate that the Lord has permitted me and my wife, Traci, to also be dedicated to serving people *after* birth and throughout their lives as I have also witnessed many other Christians doing the same. But still, *the perception was out there.*

How and why is it out there? Recall one of the characteristics observed by Schaeffer above while analyzing secularism: *a widening gap between the rich and the poor.* The disparities of course go far beyond economics, but *a widening gap* might be an apropos general diagnosis. Dr. Koenig reminded me as we launched our talk that it "seems like problems are '*far out there*' in the world, [but] truth is, there are *two worlds.*" Dr. Koenig was taking me into the realm of a new consideration: how to bring the love of Jesus Christ through engagement with *those who are broken.* She reminded me that God is always cognizant of this very thing and this also explains why—by the way—God gave us the Gospel of Luke. It is the Gospel for *the disenfranchised,* as in *those lacking rights or privileges,* or if we use Dr. Koenig's preferred term: *the broken.*

Look past Social Problems and See the *Person*

Dr. Koenig started to shape a perspective for me: "When we look past *social problems,* how do very personal things like divorce, single-parent

---

[150] Kristen Koenig, interview by author, Concordia University, Irvine, California, December 17, 2019.

families, 'Kaleidoscope' families,[151] children only related to one parent, multiple marriages so that sometimes a child only has one blood relationship in a household, *affect people*?" Dr. Koenig was increasing my awareness. I felt convicted that while I was immensely aware of the social problems she had mentioned, I had spent less time considering the *personal and individualized effects*.

"For example," Dr. Koenig continued, "opioid addiction: We can write people off and say, 'do the crime, do the time,' or 'you've made your bed, now lie in it,' but there's not a lot of grace out there toward brokenness, and culturally, we have a warped way of viewing things. We say either:

1. *'It's not my business, so it's not my problem'* . . . what comes out of individualism and moral subjectivity, or on the flip side,

2. *'I'm really sorry, but what can I do about it?'*"

Dr. Koenig continued, "As Christians, we can't ignore the broken. We need *acts of compassion*." Her words took me back to Hauerwas and Willimon: "By focusing on practices we are trying to find ways to help one another [as Christians] resist the tendency for Christianity to become a matter of belief, of values."[152] In addition, the same authors actually reached back to Schaeffer, comparing our culture to that of Rome: "Once Christians, however, had made peace with Rome they began to think that salvation had to do [exclusively] with their inner life."[153]

Dr. Koenig, however, wasn't just going to speak platitudes, but instead offered this challenge: "It's easy to think in terms of being the *Good Samaritan, but*—and I don't know what you'll think of this, Pastor [as she wondered if what she was about to say might offend my scriptural understanding]—*the Good Samaritan is Jesus, not Americans . . . we are all in the ditch*!" I was interviewing a sociologist, but she had just

---

[151] As in constantly shifting and rapidly changing families.

[152] Hauerwas and Willimon, *Where Resident Aliens Live*, 20.

[153] Hauerwas and Willimon, *Where Resident Aliens Live*, 33.

betrayed her exceptional theology, as this interpretation has long been with the Church that is Christ-centered.

All Are Broken

Dr. Koenig exclaimed—not wanting this main point to sneak by: *"We are all broken!* We cannot behave as if we are swooping in and fixing brokenness. We need ethical and morally responsible responses so that we are in *relationship* with people." As far as I was concerned, Dr. Koenig was affirming the entire premise of the **engagement triangle**.

Dr. Koenig was ready to elaborate: "I don't know if you've heard of Jeffrey Brown, who is a Baptist minister in Boston, but he was doing his thing with volunteers, programs, sermons, but then, what pushed him over the edge was a fourteen-year-old who was shot one block from the church. . . . He had been running to church, but the church was closed, and Pastor Brown realized that he was not in relationship; he was doing *to them*, [and was] not *in relationship*. He had to get into the neighborhood . . . *they* are the subject-matter experts. . . . He started *listening* . . . and realized that [these broken ones] were some of the smartest people he knew."

Again, I was feeling convicted. How often had I done *ministry from afar*? Dr. Koenig said, "We are called to be in *relationship* with our neighbor." When I heard her say this, I asked myself silently, "And who is my neighbor?" It wasn't enough to say "everyone" for theological points, but Dr. Koenig was more specific: "The people right there with us."

Recalibrating Our View of Neighbor

"We need to recalibrate how we view our neighbor." Dr. Koenig was now explaining the lenses needed for good engagement. She told me a story about a Christian trying way too hard to evangelize through this philosophical or that theological argument. The Christian had to be admonished by another Christian observing their frustrated efforts: "Get out of the way of the Holy Spirit!" Dr. Koenig elaborated on three things we can do to help:

1. **"Notice that people need help.** We need to pay attention to people, pray for them, see how they're hurting. The more people

internalize, the worse it gets, so paying attention is very important. Being attentive, we remind ourselves that we [shortchange] the idea of *help*. True care comes with sacrifice, and sacrifice hurts. Americans have a cheap version of *care*. In our families, we will sacrifice, but bridging out, we make donations!

2. **"Explain our behavior better [when we don't help]:** How can thirty-some people witness a horrible crime and not call the police? There are of course situational factors, but we probably would have done the same. We need to understand our own fallibility . . . know the pitfalls we fall into . . . [we reduce our "help" to]: "I'm going to sermonize you, judge you, tell you that your lifestyle is not godly, feel sorry for you, pity you," but none of these things are empathy.

3. **"Take responsibility:** This is where sacrifice comes in. We can't just do a drive-by."

I queried, "These points sound good, but how do we even begin?" Dr. Koenig understood the tall order, but she also knew the first step: "We have to realize that all of us have something broken in us. Reach into your own brokenness first. Before you take the speck out of your neighbor's eye, take the log out of your own" (see Matthew 7:3). I was inspired by her answer because she took me back to Holy Scripture. In addition to her reference to St. Matthew's Gospel, I had 1 John 1:8–9 ringing in my ears: "If we say we have no sin, we deceive ourselves, and the truth is not in us. If we confess our sins, He is faithful and just to forgive us our sins and to cleanse us from all unrighteousness." Indeed, we need to begin with ourselves, or as Dr. Koenig had put it, "Reach into [our] own brokenness first." Again, it isn't about "getting into the same boat," but confessing "I'm already in it" with my fellow sinners while knowing I am also loved by Jesus, just like the person I'm called to engage—and not only in my words. Dr. Koenig also reminded me of James 2:17: "So also faith by itself, if it does not have works, is dead." This saying maintains the balance: "While faith in Christ *alone* saves, this faith is *never* alone." A life follows.

Not Damning Judgment, but Christ

Dr. Koenig offered some final counsel as we headed to the end of our conversation. "Ask yourself, 'What are the other factors in play?' Sometimes people grow up with a perverse version of Christianity. Sometimes we can't be the one to provide the most help and may need to set boundaries, so we also need to know our own limits. For the Christian though, we can show generosity, and we don't even have to quote Scripture. Look at lives in relationship. Don't ask how we're going to fix people, because none of this is going to get fixed, *but Christ has already done something for us.* When people bemoan the culture, we need to remind them that Jesus is bigger than the culture, the culture war, because God made the world; He's bigger than all of us, but we can't do this outside relationship. We cannot use damning judgment and drive people away. What people have done does not define them, but Christ came and died for all our sins . . . and *this* transcends time, place, and culture."

Engagement Triangle Point 3: Place and Cultural Influence

The first point of the engagement triangle is **perspective**, and when it comes to personhood, secularism in the culture tries to take God out of the equation. Christians must resist this basic move and hold to God's definition of personhood.

The second point of the engagement triangle is **people**. Remember the condition of the human soul: *incurvatus in se*—curved in on ourselves. Immersed in this condition, people are immersed in pleasures, too busy to look beyond self. Christians can do it better by entering into relationship instead of "doing ministry" from afar and in a detached way.

This leads us to the third point of the engagement triangle: **place**. Recall that this place—the world—is a place marked by individualism, relativism, and skepticism. In these two interviews, however, we were reminded that people without Christ aren't the only ones who are myopic, flighty, and inexorable. Christians are too. Dr. Chittick's counsel to fight ignorance and fear by delving in to *invest* in those with special needs, and Dr. Koenig's counsel to see the brokenness that we share with others that we might *sacrifice* for the broken, both describe life in Christ and bring God's salt and light to place.

PLACE

• CULTURE
- Resist Secularism That Wants God Out of Equation

To impact place, however, the Christian needs help. Where do we find this life of Christ that we might share with others? Rather than looking to the world, the Christian is called to look to that transcultural community within the culture: the Holy Church. This place within place, where the Holy Spirit leads God's people through Word and Sacrament to be little Christs, is needed not only for those issues in the culture *upon us* like science, politics, and personhood, but also for those issues *within us*: sexuality, addiction, and depression. To these, we now turn.

CHAPTER 9 DISCUSSION GUIDE

ENGAGING PERSONHOOD

UNCOVER INFORMATION

1. Define *person*.

2. How does Scripture substantiate that the unborn and newly born babies are real and complete *persons*?

3. If Christians misrepresent Christian teaching and life, then secularism will often say what about Christianity?

4. "If there are no absolutes by which to judge society, then _____ is _____."

5. Dr. Chittick taught us about "person-first language." Why is this important?

DISCOVER MEANING

1. What does the *image of God* mean?

2. Why should infants be baptized according to Scripture?

3. Why is the answer to question 3 under "Uncover Information" above a non sequitur, something that doesn't follow logically?

4. What did the Lord Jesus mean by "the love of many will grow cold"?

5. Dr. Koenig says, "We need to recalibrate how we view our neighbor." What does this mean?

EXPLORE IMPLICATIONS

1. If God has created and redeemed all people (and He has), then what does this say about the value and importance of every human life?

2. What are the implications of secularism against Christianity and therefore personhood?

3. If God's Word is removed, then how will the understanding of personhood be affected?

4. "To reject God is to reject the treatment of persons." Agree or disagree? Why?

5. What does it look like to *invest* (Dr. Chittick) and to *sacrifice* (Dr. Koenig) with respect to heartfelt engagement?

PART IV:

ENGAGEMENT

TRIANGLE APPLIED

TO CULTURAL

ISSUES WITHIN US

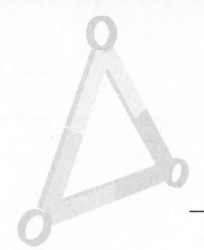

CHAPTER 10:
ENGAGING SEXUALITY

Small Catechism

The Sixth Commandment: You shall not commit adultery.

What does this mean? We should fear and love God so that we lead a sexually pure and decent life in what we say and do, and husband and wife love and honor each other.

Large Catechism

The Sixth Commandment: In general and in all conditions it is solemnly commanded by God that men and women, who were created for marriage, shall be found in this estate. Yet there are some exceptions (although few) whom God has especially set apart. They are not fit for the married estate. Or there are individuals whom He has released by a high, supernatural gift so that they can maintain chastity without this estate [Matthew 19:11–12]. For where nature has its course—since it is given by God—it is not possible to remain chaste without marriage [1 Corinthians 7]. For flesh and blood remain flesh and blood. The natural desire and excitement have their course without delay or hindrance, as everybody sees and feels. In order, therefore, that it may be easier in some degree to avoid inchastity, God has commanded the estate of marriage. In this way everyone may have his proper portion and be satisfied with it. Yet God's grace is also required in order that the heart may be pure.[154]

The Sixth Petition: To feel temptation is, therefore, a far different thing from consenting or yielding to it. . . . Such feeling, as long as it is against our will and we would rather be rid of it, can harm no one. For if we did not feel it, it could not be called a temptation. But we consent to it when we give it the reins and do not resist or pray against it.[155]

Apology of the Augsburg Confession

First, Genesis 1:28 teaches that people were created to be fruitful, and that one sex should desire the other in a proper way.[156]

Engagement Triangle Point 1: Perspective and Approach

The Issue behind the Issue: Rejecting God's Creation of Male and Female, and "the Gift of the Other"

I was truly blessed to be able to interview Vicar (pastoral candidate) Brian Barlow, who has specialized in outreach to those he refers to as having *a gender-broken identity*. He has invested more than twenty years serving those who struggle with relational and sexual brokenness. He is also the regional director for a para ministry in the Pacific Southwest District of The Lutheran Church—Missouri Synod, which offers hope to the gender-broken, pastors, church leaders, and parents of people who are gay and transgender.[157] Before we dove into the actual interview, he shared his own story with me.

---

[154] LC I 211–12.

[155] LC III 107–8.

[156] Ap XXIII 7.

[157] Brian Barlow, interview by author, Lake Forest, California, December 30, 2019.

When Brian was young—only twenty years old—he had been going through a season of real confusion about his sexual identity. He enlisted the help of a counselor who was trained, intelligent, had earned a degree, and was assuredly trustworthy (or so he thought). When Brian looks back on what happened, he knows it didn't have to happen, but unfortunately, it did. He needed someone to talk to him, to help him unpack his feelings, and to point him back to his masculinity. Instead, the counselor was destructive.

Brian recounted, "This 'Christian' counselor [so-called], divorced of reason and understanding—and I thought at the time on account of his title that he was smarter than me; I was very vulnerable—anyway, this guy allowed me to share my story for four months . . . about the wanderings and fears of a young man's heart and my insecurity about my sexuality. I struggled with my gender identity . . . and same-sex attraction. . . . This counselor said, 'Go to the bars . . . Maybe that's how God created you.' *That was like someone punched me.*" Vicar Barlow had followed the counselor's advice. He continued, "When I acted out of hopelessness . . . and went into gay bars in Chicago, it was the worse time of my life. . . . All of it was perversion of anything good of how to treat one another: you divide and conquer and take what you can get. My world became very dark and depraved."

There is, of course, much more to Vicar Barlow's story, but suffice it to say that he was released from bondage through the Gospel of Jesus Christ. His life has changed, and he will be the first one to tell you that there really is *transformation* that follows justification. He will also tell you that he is still a sinner, but now instead of living in darkness, he lives in the light of Christ, and the Lord has led him to serve others in amazing ways.

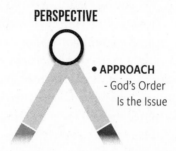

PERSPECTIVE

• **APPROACH**
- God's Order
  Is the Issue

When we got to analyzing sexuality and the perspective needed to engage people immersed in sexual confusion, the vicar started with a bold statement that caught me off guard: "It's not about sexuality, but rather a *relational* issue that translates into, 'I don't know how to deal with the gift of the *other.*'" I was a little taken aback. After all, how can issues like homosexuality, lesbianism, and gender dysphoria—terms and labels that we use from the culture to identify varying departures from God's original creation—*not* be about sexuality? As we continued to interact, I began to realize where the vicar was coming from: of course, acts and lifestyles that violate the Sixth Commandment are about sexuality, and yet I began to realize that the vicar's assertion contained truth.

Wait a minute! Which is it then? Are we talking about sexuality or not? As a Lutheran Christian pastor-theologian well aware of the constancy of paradoxes recognized in the sacred faith (what I like to call *dualities*), the answer to "Which is it?" is "Yes!"

The world and our culture have redefined sexuality. When sin came into the world, Genesis 3 describes disruption and disunion in man's relationship with God (we hide from Him), within self (we experience shame), and toward others (through accusing others). This disruption and disunion manifest in our sexuality. When one compares the pristine creation with the fallen world, practically everything has been redefined (and not for good). McGrath points out that the condition of sin "brings with it a propensity for distortion, by which God's revelation in creation is easily changed into an idol of our own making."[158]

---

[158] McGrath, *Intellectuals Don't Need God*, 17.

Neither Holy Scripture nor the Lutheran Confessions fail to discuss sexuality in two varying contexts. With respect to the original creation from God or the new life that follows regeneration, that context is positive, to say the least. For example, from Luther's Small Catechism above, Luther wrote "sexually pure," and in the Apology of the Augsburg Confession, Philip Melanchthon wrote "one sex" to refer either to male or female. That is, *sexuality* from the good creation is *very good* (Genesis 1:31). Whenever we are discussing God-given sexuality, make no mistake about it—we are talking about sexuality as it ought to be.

On the other hand, Scripture also discusses things relating to sexuality that give way to *disunity* and *distortions*. And while these are contrasted to *true* sexuality, these things are now about sexuality *gone astray*. Something else is going on. There is a bigger and deeper problem in the background: namely, *straying from God's creation*. I like the way Schlossberg describes the problem in terms of sexuality having been removed from morality.[159] This leads us to the progression pointed out in the prior chapter (with a little longer chain reaction for our present consideration): *Remove God, remove God's Word, remove God's Law, remove right and wrong, remove morals, and what is "sexuality" when this happens?*

There are six places in the Holy Scriptures that discuss the depraved version of sexuality that sin has redefined: three main texts from the Old Testament, and three main texts from the New Testament:

Genesis 19:4–8	Romans 1:24–28
Leviticus 18:22	1 Corinthians 6:9–10
Leviticus 20:13	1 Timothy 1:10

The remnant of "sexuality" that remains is now about natural desires emanating from the sinful heart. Christ the Lord described many sins that come "out of the heart," and "sexual immorality" is one of them (Matthew 15:19). Sexuality when expressed from the sinful heart is now all about the individual as one who stands independent

---

[159] Schlossberg, *Idols for Destruction*, 171.

and apart from God (individualism). Sexuality is now defined by the popular opinions of people in the culture (relativism). In this context, even the word *sexuality* can seem passé as the world ventures further and further from male and female and denies the way sexuality was first given to us by God (skepticism).

Are Right and Wrong Real?

So, the issue is this: Is sexuality whatever people make it? Or is it defined by God? In other words, *"Do right and wrong really exist?"*[160] William Lane Craig helps us to avoid underestimating this question, for a simple reason: "Morality isn't just in your mind, it's real."[161] Furthermore, if morality *is* real, then it *can't be subjective* based on human opinion.[162]

C. S. Lewis, of course, was masterful on this point: "Whenever you find a man who says he does not believe in a real Right and Wrong, you will find the same man going back on this a moment later."[163] What did Lewis mean? He meant that even while people *behave* a certain way while claiming they do not believe in a real right and wrong, they *still* have a sense of what they ought to do and what they ought not do.[164] He calls this the Law of Human Nature or the Moral Law. At the same time, all people break this law constantly. But why should this be *real*? Because this oughtness, sense of right and wrong, and law of morality comes from God. But in today's culture, people assert that "right and wrong are not matters of *fact*, but matters of *taste*."[165]

This instinct and overarching feeling based on human experience as opposed to any objective standard is the new *sexuality*. In this way, Vicar Barlow is 100 percent correct. The *real* issue is that we've exchanged the truth of God for a lie so that now, as the vicar put it, *"We don't know how to deal with the gift of the other."* That is, man and

---

[160] William Lane Craig, *Hard Questions, Real Answers* (Wheaton, IL: Crossway Books, 2003), 130.

[161] Craig, *Hard Questions*, 130.

[162] Craig, *Hard Questions*, 131.

[163] Lewis, *Mere Christianity*, 6.

[164] Lewis, *Mere Christianity*, 8, 17.

[165] Craig, *Hard Questions*, 131.

woman have lost the original sexuality God gave to them for each other and—due to sin—*ceased being what God originally created them to be.*

But here's the thing: the core problem described above (straying from God's original order in creation) is not a problem confined to a segment in society but is a problem that is *universal among all people.*

All Have Violated the Sixth Commandment, and All Are Guilty of Breaking the Entire Law

We Christians have much to repent of when it comes to how we engage with those who are loved by God just as much as anyone and are dealing with issues regarding sexuality. We have lost our view of the universality of sin. Remember: Christians are already in the same boat—so to speak—with all other sinners. To be a Christian does not mean that your sin now smells better than someone else's. To put it another way, the sinful nature (itself) is never converted. Yes, Christians receive a new spirit, but the old flesh doesn't vacate even while we are enabled by the Holy Spirit through Christ's Word and Sacraments to resist it.

But as for this sin piece that is like a spiritual disease in the hearts of people: welcome to the club. Given this, if a Christian looks down upon anyone struggling with sexual sin, then that Christian needs to hear God's Word: "For all have sinned and fall short of the glory of God" (Romans 3:23). And, "For whoever keeps the whole law but fails in one point has become guilty of all of it" (James 2:10).

What is more, there isn't a Christian alive who hasn't violated the Sixth Commandment in one form or another, either by sins of commission or omission. Recall the meaning of "You shall not commit adultery" from the Small Catechism: "*We should fear and love God so that we lead a sexually pure and decent life in what we say and do, and husband and wife love and honor each other.*" Who has been completely sexually pure? Who has experienced sexuality—whether thought about, talked about, or acted on—in such a way that it has always been decent? What husband or wife has never fallen short in the "love and honor" department? Which Christians have lusted in their hearts? Which of them committed fornication before marriage? Which one of them have never watched what they should not have watched? And which of them have not kept the marriage bed pure? The Church is full of Sixth Commandment breakers.

There are some who can better help us understand our need to be more considerate of these things. In addition to Vicar Brian Barlow, I was privileged to interview two more brothers in Christ regarding their own homosexuality or gender dysphoria. In addition, this chapter presents a portion of an interview with a Christian sister named Heather Ruesch. Heather has *not* lived in a sexually immoral lifestyle but has been led by God to serve people struggling with sexual idols. Of the three brothers in Christ, however, *all* confess Christ, and by God's grace, *no longer practice* homosexual behavior or lean toward compromises regarding gender identity. One of them, however, made me more aware of how some Christians can make matters worse. My brother in Christ—the first of whom will remain anonymous—shared this:

> I know what it feels like to live in isolation, feeling like you're the only one. I've asked, "Why me?" and have prayed, "Please, Lord, don't give up on me." I have not presumed to be better, but I have often presumed to be worse. I've been around Christians when they discover someone is attracted to the same sex; they start acting disturbed, judgmental, surprised, and shocked . . . and then they start backing away. I had an old friend who became a pastor. I knew him before he became a pastor, and he was aware of my sin, but years later when we were once again face-to-face, he became standoffish. . . . We act like [sexual sin] is worse than others, and it's easy for some Christians to say things like, "You should know better" or "You shouldn't do that," et cetera. But this isn't helpful when you don't understand about shame (though some homosexuals have no shame).

The ironic thing about my brother in Christ who shared this with me is that he is one of the most mature Christians I've ever met. He would probably blush if he heard me say that, and wonder what I may have been drinking, but it is true. Lewis once wrote, "When a man is getting better he understands more and more clearly the evil that is still left in him. When a man is getting worse he understands his own badness less and less."[166] My dear brother in Christ has been given much clarity and demonstrates the work of the Holy Spirit to rely less on himself and more on Christ.

"Sins against His Own Body" (1 Corinthians 6:18)

Still, you've probably picked up on the tenor of what has here been presented in terms of being in the "same boat" and the universality of sin. But nevertheless, can we really say that sexual sins are not any worse than other sins? Of course, in the sense that *all* sins reveal a depraved state that leads to death, it is true—again, in *this* sense, no single sin is worse than another. Is this, however, true *in every* sense?

There is probably one Scripture especially pertinent to the question, 1 Corinthians 6:18: "Flee from sexual immorality. Every other sin a person commits is outside the body, but the sexually immoral person sins against his own body." The most glaring reason why sins of sexual immorality acted out by Christians are especially egregious is *because they involve sinning against the body of Christ's temple since Christians are members of the Church.* And while the context of 1 Corinthians 6:12–20 emphasizes the Body of Christ, the Church, St. Paul is also making a case by extension that the individual's physical body ("temple" of each believer) can be defiled (1 Corinthians 6:19).[167] What is more, sins of the body in sexual immorality sin *with another person in their body.* Lockwood states flatly, "Not only does the sexually immoral person sin against the church and her spiritual union with the Lord (6:15–17), but he also defiles his own body [not to mention the violation of another's body]."[168]

My other dear brother in Christ who wished to remain anonymous made it very personal: "1 Corinthians 6 and 'sins against the body' . . . those who have experienced it, we know it to be true. It's different

---

[166] Lewis, *Mere Christianity*, 93.

[167] Lockwood, *1 Corinthians*, 220.

[168] Lockwood, *1 Corinthians*, 220.

because you can't undo it. Once you've given yourself to someone that way, you've sinned against yourself. It's true. The moment [after the sexual sin occurs] you hate yourself, and you don't like the other person. Then comes instant shame and guilt . . . and self-loathing."

So, how is the Christian to think of these things? This sin—and let this be lucid—*Christ took it and put it on Himself.* If it is the most horrendous curse, then yes indeed, Christ took it "by becoming a curse for us" (Galatians 3:13). This sin, too, is covered by the all-powerful blood of Christ, stronger than *any* sin. This sin is *not* the unforgivable sin that rejects the Gospel (Matthew 12:32). For all who tremble and are afraid: they must know that this sin *has also been forgiven by the accomplished Gospel.* This is what faith knows as it clings to Jesus!

Remember What We Said about Obsessing

We must, however, still answer the question, "But what should the Christian do with this revelation?" The Christian is not called to obsess about the sin, *but rather to be concerned about the shame.* We already know that "most people are aware that something is missing from their lives."[169] But what of the suffering homosexual? It is so often the case: "The last thing the suffering . . . may need [in application to any acted-out sexual immorality] is any further application of the Law; often he will already be painfully aware of his sin."[170]

So, we ask the question again: "What should the Christian do with this revelation?" The answer is to be full of *compassion*; *to be as Christ is toward sinners.* Besides, at the end of the day—after all the analysis of this or that sin—all should be like St. Paul, who called himself the *worst* of sinners (1 Timothy 1:15) and who explained, "But I received mercy for this reason, that in me, as the foremost, Jesus Christ might display His perfect patience as an example to those who were to believe in Him for eternal life" (v. 16). Each individual sinner should be convinced of being the worst—since no one else has a front-row seat to all your sins (at least the ones you're aware of). That alone should cause

---

[169] McGrath, *Intellectuals Don't Need God,* 15.

[170] Lockwood, *1 Corinthians,* 209.

the Christian to forget about comparisons. This is the Church's call toward those who have sinned sexually: *compassion.*

Distinguish between Homosexual Desire and Practice

One last point to round out **perspective** in the engagement triangle. We have already considered above in connection to Matthew chapter 15 that the sinful heart is the source for all sin, but it is always important to recognize the difference between *inclination* versus *behavior.* As we have said, all sin is grievous just as all sin is damnable, *but* sin perpetuated can lead to a hardened heart or a besetting sin that leads someone beyond repentance. This potentiality of course goes beyond homosexuality, lesbianism, and transgender identity:

> That a person may sometimes be overtaken by homosexual thoughts does not justify indulging those thoughts and acting on them. By way of comparison, we may consider the more common human propensity toward adulterous desires. These desires are condemned by Jesus as sinful in themselves (Mt 5:28). But to indulge them to the point of physical adultery involves the person in far more serious spiritual bondage and social damage, both to himself ("the one fornicating sins against his body," 1 Cor 6:18) and to others. The biblical condemnations of homosexuality focus their spotlight on indulgence in homosexual *behavior.*[171]

Lockwood rounds out his important distinction: "Therefore, the passage [1 Corinthians 6:9–10 on those including the sexually immoral not inheriting God's kingdom] is best interpreted as referring to *practicing* homosexuals, *practicing* adulterers, and so on, rather than to all persons who have immoral *thoughts*—which would include *all* people!"[172] William Lane Craig makes a crucial point related to this where the term *orientation* refers to *the thoughts and desires that come*

---

[171] Lockwood, *1 Corinthians*, 204.
[172] Lockwood, *1 Corinthians*, 206.

from temptation: "What the [Word of God] condemns is homosexual actions or behavior, not having a homosexual orientation."[173]

This being the case, Christians are not good stewards of their time when they pursue debates as to whether one is born with *x* sexual predisposition or not. As Craig points out, "The important thing is not how you *got* your orientation, but what you *do with it*."[174]

Engagement Triangle Point 2: People and Attitude

Start with Love

When it comes to the second point on the engagement triangle—**people**—you might recall that this is the point that urges us to find *common ground*. Without question, it is only the most naive Christian who will say they share no common ground with those practicing sexual immorality. This is simply not true.

The immediate common ground we share is that as sinners we are also among the broken. Sinners know they fall short of God's standard. Recall, who has *not* broken the Sixth Commandment? Who is *not* guilty of breaking them all (James 2:10)? But there is also another thing the Christian shares: we desire to love and to be loved. I've grown very close to a parishioner who has been through unspeakable sexual trauma. One day while counseling, she screamed in frustration, "I just want someone to *love* me!"

PEOPLE

• ATTITUDE
- Emphasize Love &
  Coming alongside People

---

173 Craig, *Hard Questions*, 134.

174 Craig, *Hard Questions*, 134.

And who cannot relate to *that*? But as you might know, there are many variations of love: romantic love, the love of friends, and the love within families. The love people need most, though, is sacrificial, unconditional. That love is *agape*. But some might struggle: "How exactly do I show *this* love?" Before exhausting ourselves as we brainstorm, let's keep it simple even as the answer is also profound: Our goal is to love as Christ loved. It is not as hard as some might think. Begin with His incarnation. What did He do? He took on our flesh and tented among us (John 1:14). He entered our lives. He was and is *there for us*.

Coming alongside People

Heather Ruesch is the author of the book *Sexuality Mentality*. The Lord has given her a heart to reach young people who are immersed in our culture of the world's version of sexuality. I was thankful for the window of opportunity I had to speak with her.[175] She is as full of Christlike compassion as she is gifted with both a high IQ and EQ. I asked if she might share with me what she means by *sexuality mentality*. She was ready to answer. "When people get immersed in sexuality mentality, it becomes an idol, a driving force, an addiction." Needless to say, I couldn't wait to ask her the next question, "How does a Christian effectively engage a person in this situation?"

She replied, "It depends on the individual and the circumstances. . . . We are uniquely made, therefore uniquely attacked! First, look beyond whatever it is that they are identifying with at the time, even the pain, whatever their idol is. I'm trying to look beyond that. We all have idols . . . to find our value in. Often it's sexuality or addiction or vanity, power, abuse, pain . . . the person identifies with something. I want to look beyond that. The behavior is an indication of something deeper."

I needed some specifics. "Got it, but when you say you 'look beyond,' what exactly are you doing? What does it look like?"

Heather: "*I come alongside them* to find the root cause. . . . I'm not just going to look at the thing [the external idol], but I need to go to the *core*. What is making this person feel worthless, alone? What's causing

---

175 Heather Ruesch, interview by author, December 14, 2019.

them not to know their value in Christ? I ignore the behavior when I'm seeking to come alongside somebody."

I was intrigued by this description, *coming alongside someone.* I felt a little self-conscious about narrowing this down as I was, but I knew it was going to be worth it: "Coming alongside someone?"

Heather clarified: "As an analogy: my daughter fell and hurt herself, so *I got down on the ground, looked at the wound, and asked, 'How did this happen?'* It's hard to come alongside someone, to bend down and be near them . . . *to be in proximity.* I'm engaged in their daily life; I am *interested in them.* Then I share my story so that eventually they can share their story with me."

In our confession as evangelical Christians, we are pretty cognizant that we aren't the ones who change anyone in engagement. It is only the Holy Spirit alone who calls, gathers, and enlightens, as the Small Catechism says in the explanation of the Third Article. Heather affirmed this biblical theology, but then said something else that reminded me that the Lord does indeed *choose to work through His servants.* Heather described this beautifully as I continued to get a better picture of coming alongside people.

"We have to recognize that we are not the one who changes hearts, *but we are the one through whom God shows relationship,* and we can speak truth," she said. "Just offer a relationship and love and God will use us. Relationships are complicated, but be in proximity, slow down, *and be with them.* . . . We can share our bad stories! . . . It's not through the great times and high moments that we bond, but through the hard times. That's when we get close to people, sharing fears and struggles. This is how we gain a sense of camaraderie. So much comes from humility when people become willing to share their story. This is when engagement reaches people: when we bring the love of Christ to the whole person."

Not Condoning but Walking With

I also received tremendous insight from my second brother in Christ remaining anonymous—the same one who described his experience of 1 Corinthians 6 above—regarding how Christians should engage those active in a sexually immoral lifestyle. Before outlining his counsel, however, it's important to share that the words that flowed from this Christian man were *astounding*. They were filled with the discovery of grace, the sufficiency of Christ, and the joyful willingness to bear his cross for Christ. And it occurred to me: we ought never underestimate how those caught in any sin might be transformed by God to live full of faith in Christ and mighty in Christian service within the Church and to the world. I am humbled that I get to call him and my other two brothers in Christ my friends.

He jumped in when I asked him specifically about how the Christian can engage: "The verse I use is 1 Corinthians 13:1–3. Start in love. We love our neighbor regardless of presuppositions. Loving the least is what God did. He spent His time with the dregs of the culture like tax collectors and prostitutes."

I liked the way he began, but often in our culture, *love* can be used as a synonym for *condoning*, so I wondered about how my brother in Christ might qualify what he just said. So, I asked, "Brother, would you elaborate a little more about *starting in love . . . regardless of presuppositions?*"

He was ready to elaborate: "Loving doesn't mean we accept sin . . . love the man, not the actions. The problem is that people [caught up in sexual sin] get the impression that Christians don't really care, but just showing up can make a big difference. When we do this, we just accept them for who they are and not for what they do. A lot grow up in the church and that's why so many just want to turn it off—sexual desire or being gay—and why drug use is so rampant. How do you deal with it [same-sex desire] if you're told 'you're not gay' and 'you'll grow out of it'? When parents don't accept it, then why would you trust the church? I also avoided the church because I was mad at God for 'creating' me gay and then telling me that what came to me naturally was immoral. Unfortunately, I didn't understand all sin comes naturally to human beings. I wish I could have learned that sooner. But if we're able to love unconditionally, accept them for who they are . . . until they can trust the Church, they can't trust Christ. We desire to love God because of these people who didn't know you from Adam [but] loved you anyway." Later in this interview, he elucidated on what he meant by "unconditional love."

> The key is encouragement without condoning. We can say, "I'm not condoning, but we are friends so I will be there for you. I can't condone, but I will support." In other words, we balance love and integrity: "We love you and want to serve you." The balance is to love and to retain the truth at the same time. So, there is a difference between accepting and condoning. This is where we walk a fine line.

I thought the "balance" he was describing epitomized *engagement*, and I viewed his verbal portrait as showing Jesus, the One who ate with tax collectors and sinners (Matthew 9:11). He never condoned their sin, but He *accepted their person by joining their company and extending His grace and service.*

I had to round out this line of thought by asking my brother in the Lord, "As we strive for this balance, what are some basic things *we should say* and things *we should avoid saying*?" He shifted and I could tell he was about to provide important words: "We should acknowledge that we are on the same playing field and sinners like everyone else, by acknowledging that we all 'have a past' and that we're sinners too. Things to *avoid* saying are things that discredit their experience with sexuality. Never tell someone that they will grow out of it, or that it is just a phase. Instead, remember that everyone at some point in their life has been vulnerable and needed affirmation . . . everyone needs someone. If you can be that one person that someone else can get love from, then take the opportunity to be His light that shines through us. Most importantly, just show up. If we're consistent in just being there, we don't even necessarily need to know what to say. Look for that chance to ask them back, 'Have you ever stopped to think why I didn't ask you about your sin? It's because I know. I'm a sinner too!' This is what might open the door for the Gospel."

The Gift of the Other Revisited

During our inspiring time together, Vicar Barlow had emphasized *the gift of the other*. If you recall, this is about stepping away from the world's fallen version of sexuality and returning to God's intention for male and female. As the vicar reminded me in his interview, "You can't remove God's intent for humanity." Gospel and creation run together. The Gospel is for those who also confess their sin of turning away from the will of God, especially as it is evident in creation.

Vicar pointed out: "If someone is using their feelings as their only tool to evaluate reality, then they . . . can make a conscious decision to ignore something that is true. [By nature] we want to take away safety and what is most important [to those rejecting God's will] is to have pleasure." As Vicar Barlow made abundantly clear, however, there is no "gay Gospel" versus "heterosexual Gospel." Instead—as he supplied a golden quote, "Good News rolls out in embracing and confessing the good of creation." He was emphasizing our need to return to the beauty of male and female . . . to the gift of the other.

In saying this, and before continuing, we must acknowledge that Christians have testified differently (and continue to do so) about God's healing and transformation in their lives. Some have said that delivery from sins of sexuality can take on full restoration of gender identity and heterosexual desire, while other Christians have warned against this position that might lead another to be convinced that they can never be a Christian. There is much at stake.

There are theological reasons for both views with respect to 1 Corinthians 6:11: "And such were some of you [who practiced, for example, sexual immorality, v. 9]. But you were washed, you were sanctified, you were justified in the name of the Lord Jesus Christ and by the Spirit of our God." Lockwood helps as he points out "that the grace of God has the power to overcome all sins. Regardless of what factors may be involved, God's grace 'in the name of the Lord Jesus Christ' and 'the Spirit of our God' (6:11) are able to defeat those sins."[176]

---

[176] Lockwood, *1 Corinthians*, 201.

What is important here is not to force an unnecessary either-or, but to realize what is essential to the 1 Corinthians 6:11 text: *God's sanctified people are no longer mastered by sin. What is most important—regardless of desire or no desire—is that the practice of sexual sin is forsaken through repentance.* For the Christian, sinful sexual desire is drowned in Baptism and daily crucified. The Christian now sees that the old life is so repulsive that the temptation to turn back to it is preposterous. Conversely, the great blessings of the new life are held onto with increasing tenacity.

Vicar Barlow reminds us to daily return to confessing God's order and design for male and female. When the old life beckons, he says "don't be captivated by it." Instead, he says, "don't look back." What encourages this kind of mentality? God helps us, and He is "able to do far more abundantly than all that we ask or think, according to the power at work within us" (Ephesians 3:20).

In the meantime, we are spared from an either-or situation. Perhaps what comes closer to actual experience among God's sanctified people is *not* one or the other, but perhaps a little bit of both. Allow me to offer an analogy. When Jesus raised Lazarus from the dead, Lazarus experienced a 180-degree turnaround: he was dead, but then made alive again. We can't get any more transformational than that! However, as great as this was, dear Lazarus—while having been given the unspeakably amazing experience of resurrection before the final resurrection—had to experience a terrible hardship a second time: he had to die *again*. Indeed, the truth of transformation is somewhere closer to dying and rising. And wouldn't you know it, this is what Christians do by returning to their Holy Baptism into Christ day in and day out. Lockwood points out, "Paul does not say whether this means they no longer had any homosexual thoughts or desires, but their actual behavior no longer included any homosexual activity."[177]

In Vicar Barlow's own life—when his sexual identity was covered in darkness—he had rejected the good of male and female. Today, he testifies to his transformation, which—for him—led him to holy

---

[177] Lockwood, *1 Corinthians*, 209.

marriage with his wife, Nichole. He had once been taught to think that he was created less than male while relating better to the feminine. Today, he celebrates the male and female as never before. He testifies to the fact that being married has taught him how intrinsically other he is from his wife. With a smile, he recounts, "I know I'm fully male when I don't understand a word she's saying!" In the meantime, he has learned about masculinity that has naturally surfaced in his life: he fights for and protects his family, and he rejoices to be the husband and father God has made him to be.

Vicar Barlow, however, also told me about someone else who has not experienced exactly what he has. Zoe did not know who or what she was, but she felt God calling her back to Him. Vicar explained, "She knew it was God but had no context. She had lived 'as a man' for forty years. The Lord opened the door, and with a new mind, she decided that she was going to change her license into her birth name. She held up her new license to me: 'I got my name back; I got my identity back.' She is still trying to understand what it means to be fully female, to know 'this is what it looks like' even while she is still not comfortable in women's clothes. But our response as a church was clear: 'We will walk with you until you see fully what God sees.'" What would *not* happen, as Vicar explained, is that the church would do what the culture does when the culture says with a sense of resignation: "Though I don't understand, they seem okay, then it's all good, so we are all okay." Such thinking does not accept the truth of God's Word but instead says that sexuality is all about what *we* want.

Offer to Pray

If you recall, it was Vicar Barlow who said, "It's not about sexuality" as we embarked on engaging sexuality and explained what that means. In the meantime, the vicar backs up his assertion in practice. He has ministered to many in the throes of sexual immorality, and when he meets people, he focuses on three things. These, indeed, might be the most valuable words we offer in this chapter:

1. Show unconditional love toward the person. If sexuality is brought up, then listen to how they feel, but don't make sexuality the core focus for engagement. Point to masculinity and femininity as God designed it whenever there is a natural opening.

2. Be present with the person from beginning to end. Listen to them and look for an opportunity (a need, worry, or concern) for prayer.

3. Ask them if you may say a prayer over *what they shared with you* (which, by the way, proved you were listening). Don't worry. Keep it simple and speak God's love and mercy in Jesus to help in every need. Remember: most people caught in sexual immorality don't need the Law. Shame is already filling the hearts of many.

I was truly moved to hear about how such an approach has served Vicar Barlow. He strives to care about and know the person standing in front of him. And then he listens, listens, and listens. If *anything* is mentioned that can be prayed over (a health concern, a job issue, the indication of stress or worry, concern for a loved one, tiredness, frustration, worry, being upset about something), regardless of what it is, if you can offer a prayer for it, *do it*! It doesn't have to be eloquent. *Just let it be loving, and let it point to God's love and mercy in Jesus!*

Engagement Triangle Point 3: Place and Cultural Influence

Culture's Legitimations

As dark and as threatening as it is, the third point in the engagement triangle—**place**—is also straightforward: both the culture and the dark spiritual forces behind it strive to remove sexuality from the realm of God to the definitions of people. The culture's legitimations for this hover around one form or another that asserts that God and faith are irrelevant.

Again—consistent with what we've discussed in other chapters—the Word of God and therefore the Law of God is denied. Sexuality then becomes about what people desire over and above what God has created. Through this, even the idea of *love* is distorted. Schlossberg opined:

> Any conception that has love without law as its ethical princi-
> ple will be relativistic and self-serving and without any means
> of arranging a priority between rival goods. There is no action
> so evil that it cannot and will not be said to be motivated by
> love. Antinomian loves [loves without Law] goes perfectly
> with autonomous man; neither can stand the shackles of law.[178]

But "shackles" is the delusion of sin and the culture's caricature of the true freedom that the Law provides. Law and freedom might seem an odd pair, but the Law is precisely what curbs the flesh from leading us to the captivity of sin. The Law teaches us to know we cannot go it alone, because if we do, we will most assuredly be led into being enslaved to sin.

PLACE

● **CULTURE**
  - Resist Distortion of Love
  & Hold to God's Reality

God's Reality *Is* Reality

The culture, however, is saying more than just "God is irrelevant," but is increasingly asserting that there is no God, period. This reminds us about the significance of what we brought out early in this volume. We are confronted by individualism, relativism, and skepticism. Being immersed in these—as we have also already discussed—the result is secularism (life without God). That's a lot of isms! But take special note

---

[178] Schlossberg, *Idols for Destruction*, 47.

of the first step: *individualism*. This is when people believe with all their hearts, souls, and minds that they need nothing else but themselves. They are self-sufficient.

Given this, we face something that God therefore permits (we may realize in retrospect) for our good: people begin to suffer and in time begin to realize their mortality. This is assuredly unpleasant, but it is at the same time the wake-up call that self-sufficiency is the lie of human history. It is often during this time that the Holy Spirit paves the way for the Gospel. Let's face it: too often, living in sexual immorality leads to many other problems that touch the body and soul. If a person is not ravaged with disease, then at the very least they will start to bear a sense of shame they have never known. This is not the time for Christians to look down on people; it is the time to have compassion on the world that is dying without God.

CHAPTER 10 DISCUSSION GUIDE

ENGAGING SEXUALITY

UNCOVER INFORMATION

1. The world and culture have done *what* regarding "sexuality"?

2. Where does the sin of sexual immorality come from?

3. William Lane Craig said, "Morality isn't just in your mind, it's _____."

4. Who has broken the Sixth Commandment? In what ways is it broken?

5. Is there a difference between homosexual desire and practice? If so, what is it?

DISCOVER MEANING

1. What does it mean that cultural sexuality has strayed from God's creation?

2. If God-created sexuality is very good, what does this mean for the Christian who seeks to honor God and respect their neighbor?

3. What did C. S. Lewis mean by the "Law of Human Nature" or "Moral Law," and who has these?

4. Why are "sins against [one's] own body" unique?

5. What does Heather Ruesch mean about the value of "coming alongside people" to get behind the external idol, driving force, or addiction?

EXPLORE IMPLICATIONS

1. If God's Word is forsaken, what will be left to determine sexuality?

2. What will happen to how sexuality is viewed if individualism, relativism, and skepticism overshadow God's Word?

3. What happens if we reject what Vicar Barlow referred to as the "gift of the other"?

4. If Christ took our sin and curse (and He did), what about the sins against one's own body (and all other sins)?

5. If we are not condoning sexual sin, but nevertheless truly love the person committing it, what does this look like?

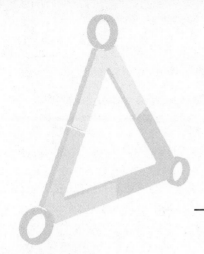

CHAPTER 11:
ENGAGING ADDICTION

Small Catechism

> **Explanation of the Second Article:** I believe that Jesus Christ
> ... redeemed me, a lost and condemned person, purchased
> and won me from all sins, from death, and from the power
> of the devil ... that I may be His own.

Creatures of Habit

As we begin this chapter, let us never forget that addiction brings
with it horrendous shame—that is, feeling lost and condemned. But a
person struggling with addiction is such a one the Gospel of Jesus Christ
was intended for. Before delving into the details on *engaging addiction*,
let it suffice for now to say that people are creatures of habit. We may
speak of *habit* within a realm that is good and pleasing to God, like the
habit—or *habitus*, the way we consistently live—of meditating on the
Word of Christ and prayer. Or we might speak of *bad habits*, and these
might include things that are very much contrary to God and to the life
He calls us to live in Christ. Either way, habits are things that people
do in general—good or bad—regularly, frequently, and consistently.

When these things get to the point of disrupting our lives in painful
and debilitating ways, we might call these *addictions*. These, too, are
habitual, but to the extent that the addiction *is in control of the person*

and not the other way around. This habit, unlike any other habit, takes on a life of its own and leads people into misery.

Engagement Triangle Point 1: Perspective and Approach

Two Kingdoms

There are many instances when the biblical and theological framework of the two kingdoms is helpful for approaching cultural issues confronting Christians. Regarding *engaging addiction* is no exception. It will be useful to consider concepts at least related to addiction from a scriptural (or kingdom of the right or churchly kingdom) perspective, but we will also review how addiction is understood in society within culture where the kingdom of the left or civic powers are in play. Working with these conceptualizations can help put the Christian in a better position to engage anyone who might be suffering from addiction.

PERSPECTIVE

• APPROACH
- Addiction Causes
Great Shame

Scriptural Considerations from the Right-Hand Kingdom

The text of 1 Corinthians 6:12 states, "'All things are lawful for me,' but not all things are helpful. 'All things are lawful for me,' but I will not be dominated by anything." St. Paul was probably addressing a slogan within pagan Greek philosophy.[179] Some Christians were adversely affected by the idea so that "they failed to understand that Christian freedom from sin and the Law's condemnation is *not* freedom *to* sin, but instead is freedom to live by the power of the Spirit in accord with God's Law (e.g., Romans 6; 13:10)."[180] The sinful flesh is capable

---

[179] Lockwood, *1 Corinthians*, 214.

[180] Lockwood, *1 Corinthians*, 215.

of being primary in a person's life so that the person is "enslaved to sin" (Romans 6:6). In this way, that person experiences death having dominion over them (Romans 6:9). "Scripture sometimes personifies sin as a tyrant, which tries to overpower its devotees and keep them subject to its authority (Gen 4:7; Rom 6:12–16)."[181]

Chrysostom helps us understand more with respect to 1 Corinthians 6:12: "Anyone who orders his desires properly remains the master of them, but once he goes beyond this limit he loses control and becomes their slave."[182] Here, the word *control* is significant. It seems that certain things—and in the context of this discussion, things that characterize sin's enslavement—can take control of a person. In this way, we see a scriptural and biblical idea related to the concept of *addiction*.

King Solomon, in writing Ecclesiastes, exclaimed, "Vanity of vanities" (1:2). He expressed this in light of man's "toils" (1:3) and "all things [being] full of weariness" (1:8). How did he know this? Evidently, he knew because there were those things he "applied [his] heart to seek and to search out" (1:13). His striving for meaning pursued wisdom (Ecclesiastes 1), self-indulgence (Ecclesiastes 2), and toil or work (Ecclesiastes 2). In all of this, King Solomon warns us about *extremes*: "Be not overly righteous, and do not make yourself too wise. Why should you destroy yourself? Be not overly wicked, neither be a fool. Why should you die before your time?" (Ecclesiastes 7:16–17). Evidently, people can go too far with respect to these things, so King Solomon concludes, "Fear God and keep His commandments, for this is the whole duty of man" (Ecclesiastes 12:13).

At the same time, to study Solomon's life is to encounter what is contrary to the wisdom in Ecclesiastes: unfathomably, he turned his life away from the Lord, who had given him all wisdom and great wealth, to worshiping idols (1 Kings 11:1–8). What could account for such a loss of self-control? This was, in truth, a kind of spiritual addiction to idolatry.

This is not surprising. Recall that when we considered **place** (the third point of the engagement triangle) in chapter 3, we said that the

---

181 Lockwood, *1 Corinthians*, 215.

182 Bray, *1–2 Corinthians*, 56.

visible culture is *not* the total environment. The Lord not only warns us about the world (1 John 2:15–17) but also warns us "against the rulers, against the authorities, against the cosmic powers over this present darkness, against the spiritual forces of evil in the heavenly places" (Ephesians 6:12).

The Book of Acts presents an intersection—in this instance—between addictive behavior and spiritual enslavement. St. Luke recorded, "As we were going to the place of prayer, we were met by a slave girl who had a spirit of divination and brought her owners much gain by fortune-telling" (Acts 16:16). She demonstrated an *obsessive* behavior by incessantly following St. Paul and crying out, and this she did "for many days" (v. 18). It was an uncontrollable pattern. When St. Paul could no longer stand it, he turned to the girl and commanded the demonic spirit to come out of her.

Even apart from a diagnosis of demonic oppression, sometimes people do what they do when overcome by sin's depravity. When St. Paul wrote in Romans that "God gave them up" (three times), referring to those who rebelled against God in crass immorality, these people continued an unabated way of life with debased minds (Romans 1:24–32).

No one should take these examples to mean that there is necessarily a one-to-one correspondence between addictive behavior and either demonic control or being under God's wrathful judgment. Indeed, even St. Paul agonized over his inner battle with sin so that he wrote, "The evil I do not want is what I keep on doing" (Romans 7:19).

Both Christians and non-Christians experience a kind of "spiritual addiction" when their encounters with sin and dark spiritual influences cause a perpetual and constant assault against them. For the Christian, this amounts to the battle or conflict against their sinful flesh, leading them to return to their Baptism on a daily basis to drown their old Adam, and to rise up in accord with their new lives in Christ.[183] For the non-Christian, this amounts to a kind of spiritual enslavement that represents a desperate need to receive the liberation that comes from the saving Gospel. For this reason alone, Christians strive to engage

---

[183] See my treatment of the Christian's inner battle in *Faith That Sees through the Culture*, chapter 7: "The Lutheran Lens—What Am I?"

for the sake of those for whom Jesus died and rose, and yet who do not know His liberation from sin, the condemnation of the Law, and death. For the Christian who feels the constancy of the battle and begins to despair (remember that St. Paul cried out, "Wretched man that I am!" [Romans 7:24]) over repeated patterns of their sinful flesh against themselves, others, and God, the Lord offers *without tiring* His consoling Word and Sacraments. But for anyone without Christ, the Christian must keep in mind that any ruinous addiction cannot be reduced to psychology or psychiatry but is attached to spiritual forces that seek the destruction of the one addicted.

Those spiritual forces against the unbeliever, however, don't look bad, but often look extraordinarily appealing under the guise of what feels like the right thing to live for. These are "counterfeit gods." Timothy Keller's book *Counterfeit Gods: The Empty Promises of Money, Sex, and Power, and the Only Hope That Matters* was a tour de force on the subject matter and will be helpful for our current consideration.

First, let's review the word *idol*. An idol is a false god loved more than *anything* or *anybody*, including more than the author of life, the one true God. Furthermore, an idol becomes something that a person *can't live without*, so that if that person lost that false idol, they would lose all hope, meaning, and purpose in life. The problem, however, is that people were not designed for false gods that cannot give life; we were created to know the one true God and have eternal life. So, in the end, an idol leads to destruction.

Second, idols really do take on many and various forms, but Keller has considered our unique culture and identified what are probably the most common counterfeit gods. One of them, of course, is money. Ecclesiastes 5:10 states, "He who loves money will not be satisfied with money." Keller diagnosis boldly, but accurately: "Money can become a spiritual addiction."[184] What about sex? "If you are too afraid of love *or* too enamored by it, it has assumed godlike power, distorting your perceptions and your life."[185] He goes on to explain how this sort of

---

[184] Timothy Keller, *Counterfeit Gods: The Empty Promises of Money, Sex, and Power, and the Only Hope That Matters* (New York: Dutton, 2009), xiii.

[185] Keller, *Counterfeit Gods*, 31.

problem aligns with addiction: "Our fears and inner barrenness make love a narcotic, a way to medicate ourselves, and addicts always make foolish, destructive choices."[186]

While money and sex might appear to be candidates for addictive behavior, can we say the same about *success*? Isn't this the backbone of our culture: to strive for the American dream? Even Christians encourage people to make full use of God's gifts. "Hard work pays off." "Don't give up on your dreams." "You can do anything if you put your mind to it." These ideas are almost as common as the air we breathe. Mary Bell is a counselor of high-performing executives that Pastor Keller quotes: "These days, the best people don't abuse alcohol. They abuse their lives. . . . An 'achievement addict' is no different from any other kind of addict."[187] In all these morphologies of idolatry, God warns us about our addictive tendencies that have a profound spiritual impact:

> The human heart takes good things like a successful career, love, material possessions, even family, and turns them into ultimate things. Our hearts deify them as the center of our lives, because, we think, they can give us significance and security, safety and fulfillment, if we attain them.[188]

All is not bleak, however, because the Lord permits us to see our idols that we may turn from them. "The way forward, out of despair, is to discern the idols of our hearts and our culture."[189] When we see these for what they are—and confess our spiritual addictions—then there is a way for change, and Keller says, "and that is through faith in the gospel."[190]

---

[186] Keller, *Counterfeit Gods*, 33.

[187] Keller, *Counterfeit Gods*, 74.

[188] Keller, *Counterfeit Gods*, xiv.

[189] Keller, *Counterfeit Gods*, xxiv.

[190] Keller, *Counterfeit Gods*, 66.

Addiction Confronted by the Means of Grace

Brandon and Chloe were lifelong Christians who were tremendously supportive of me and our congregation, and I was privileged to serve them as their pastor. They were active in the church, and we worked well together in many areas for the kingdom of God. It was clear to me that they exuded joy while holding to Christ through faith. I thanked God for them both.

One day Brandon phoned me. It sounded urgent as he apologized for the short notice. They needed to meet with me later that same day. I wanted nothing else than to be there for them, as I could hear the stress in Brandon's voice. I had no idea what they were bringing to me.

We met that evening in my study. I opened with prayer and with the typical verbal invite: "How can I serve you?" Their reaction was palpable. I could feel the anxiety flow over my desk through their hesitant facial expressions right into my heart. Then they looked at each other. I thought they might draw straws to determine who was going to tell me what was going on.

They were both educated. One was a professional with a successful company, and the other was doing a great job making their house a home with even more time volunteering in the parish. They were a team, and communication was one of their strong suits. But not tonight.

The married couple choked out a series of experienced phenomena in their home. They were afraid and needed help. Their first order of business after informing me was to discover whether I would even believe them.

When it comes to those things that might be categorized as *paranormal*, it is important that a pastor maintain a couple key points: (1) treat any report with a healthy skepticism without jumping to conclusions; and (2) treat seriously God's revelation in Holy Scripture: there are physical maladies, mental and emotional hardships, and there are *also* spiritual confrontations (just consider St. Paul's "thorn in the flesh" as recorded at 2 Corinthians 12). Brandon and Chloe were relieved that I did not treat them as though they were crazy.

The details of the phenomena are not important for me to describe; the significant thing is that it became certain that something was going on. As a pastor, I have maintained a biblical correlation: deliberate sins (or what I would consider more extreme sins of weakness) against the Lord, against oneself, and against others always have spillover or consequences that manifest. Whether those signs come out in worsening behavior or speech as in compromised morality, false confession and teaching, disruption in relationships, or even frightening phenomena as this couple had reported to me, these are often indications that something else is going on behind the scenes.

I explained this to Brandon and Chloe. My goal was *not* to highlight nor be preoccupied with the phenomena, but rather to uncover whatever needed to come under the light of God's Word. I reviewed with them the vital importance of living in Holy Baptism in such a way that we take seriously the daily discipline of the confession of our sins. We do this, of course, every time we pray the Lord's Prayer ("and forgive us our trespasses as we forgive those who trespass against us"). I then continued through the Small Catechism to elaborate not only upon the Sacrament of Holy Baptism but also upon the practice of Confession.

After this—while meeting with one of my dear parishioners—it came out. One of them was involved in a form of addictive behavior that was compromising faith and, of course, the marriage and household. Tears poured out. There was *conviction, contrition, confession,* and then I responded with *consolation* (Holy Absolution), which led to a renewed *consecration* to honor the Lord and holy marriage.[191]

The addictive behavior received help and was ultimately cut off. The house was blessed, and the Holy Sacrament of the Altar was administered to the couple in their home. I was not surprised that the ceased phenomena coincided with my parishioner receiving the Lord's healing Means of Grace. God's right-hand kingdom resources should never be underestimated in these matters. At the same time, spiritual intervention is not offered to *replace* reliable psychological resources and effective medications. *The main point here is that spiritual addictions are real,* and they touch addictions also in the realm of what—within

---

[191] Espinosa, *Faith That Sees through the Culture,* 152. This is where I have introduced what I now refer to as "the Five C's," which teach repentance in the broad sense.

the left-hand kingdom—is addressed especially by the psychological and psychiatric communities. To these considerations, we now turn.

Psychological Considerations from the Left-Hand Kingdom

The American Psychiatric Association's *Diagnostic and Statistical Manual of Mental Disorders (Fifth Edition)*, otherwise known as *DSM-5*, is the most important psychiatric diagnostic manual for clinical practice in the mental health field. Related to our current consideration, we will let *DSM-5* speak for itself through these two introductory paragraphs in its chapter entitled "Substance-Related and Addictive Disorders":

> The substance-related disorders encompass 10 separate classes of drugs: alcohol; caffeine; cannabis; hallucinogens (with separate categories for phencyclidine [or similarly acting arylcyclohexylamines] and other hallucinogens); inhalants; opioids; sedatives, hypnotics, and anxiolytics; stimulants (amphetamine-type substances, cocaine, and other stimulants); tobacco; and other (or unknown) substances. These 10 classes are not fully distinct. All drugs that are taken in excess have in common direct activation of the brain reward system, which is involved in the reinforcement of behaviors and the production of memories. They produce such an intense activation of the reward system that normal activities may be neglected. Instead of achieving reward system activation through adaptive behaviors, drugs of abuse directly activate the reward pathways. The pharmacological mechanisms by which each class of drugs produces reward are different, but the drugs typically activate the system and produce feelings of pleasure, often referred to as a "high." Furthermore, individuals with lower levels of self-control, which may reflect impairments of brain inhibitory mechanisms, may be particularly predisposed to develop substance use disorders, suggesting that the roots of substance use disorders for some persons can be seen in behaviors long before the onset of actual substance use itself.

In addition to the substance-related disorders, this chapter also includes gambling disorder, reflecting evidence that gambling behaviors activate reward systems similar to those activated by drugs of abuse and produce some behavioral symptoms that appear comparable to those produced by the substance use disorders. Other excessive behavioral patterns, such as Internet gaming, have also been described, but the research on these and other behavioral syndromes is less clear. Thus, groups of repetitive behaviors, which some term *behavioral addictions*, with such subcategories as "sex addiction," "exercise addiction," or "shopping addiction," are not included because at this time there is insufficient peer-reviewed evidence to establish the diagnostic criteria and course descriptions needed to identify these behaviors as mental disorders.[192]

Basic Principles for Engaging People with Addictions

To absorb this information from both the biblical and psychological perspectives can seem intimidating, but I would like to encourage you at this point. There is much good that the engaging Christian can do to serve someone struggling with addiction. These are basic, but crucial principles to keep in mind, as substantiated by the two experts interviewed below:

1. People living with addiction often live with extreme shame.

2. Regardless of the severity of the disorder, God's Word is still efficacious and should never be underestimated.

3. In spite of denial and the lying that accompanies it, every effort should be made to share Christ's compassion and the Gospel.

---

[192] American Psychiatric Association, *Diagnostic and Statistical Manual of Mental Disorders: DSM-5*, 5th ed. (Arlington, VA: American Psychiatric Association, 2013), 485.

Engagement Triangle Point 2: People and Attitude

It's one thing to gain **perspective** on engaging addiction, the first point of the engagement triangle, but it's another to know how to proceed with engagement itself. We have recommended throughout this volume that when it comes to the second point, **people**, we strive for common ground. Unless the Christian is also confronted by similar compulsions, trying to imagine what that common ground might be can prove difficult. But there is no need to overreact. The fact of the matter is that while it might seem that people with addictions would be *the most difficult to engage*, they might be *the most receptive to engagement*.

Let's be clear: those caught in addiction will, in fact, continue to hide it and lie about it, but that doesn't mean that their sense of shame and isolation isn't real. Even if they won't come clean about their addiction, any presentation of God's unconditional love and mercy might be the most appealing message someone battling addiction can hear. The message, of course, needs to be coupled with a non-judgmental attitude and genuine compassion.

PEOPLE

● **ATTITUDE**
- Compassion Reigns Even
  in the Face of Denial & Lies

This recommended approach won't work for every addict. There will be times that, like other people, the addict will reject any attempt to engage, but that possibility should not inhibit the Christian's effort. In general, however, when you engage addiction you will encounter *people who have already been convinced of their desperate state*; that is, the Law will have done its work through the human conscience (Romans 2:15). The goal is to let the Gospel presented with compassion slowly but surely open hearts. We should not be surprised that if the addict is convinced that the Christian is trustworthy and non-judgmental, they might finally begin to talk about their struggle. After all, why do people hide? It is because they are unwilling to risk more judgment and condemnation.

Counsel from Those in the Field

I was doubly blessed to have two outstanding professionals contribute to this chapter. Dr. Roberto Flores de Apodaca is a forensic psychologist who earned his PhD at the University of Rochester, New York, in clinical psychology. In addition to working in forensics for the legal system, he also served as a full-time professor of psychology for twenty-two years at California State University, Long Beach, and then for eighteen years at Concordia University, Irvine. In addition to Dr. Flores de Apodaca, Dr. Paul Fick was a return interviewee. This time, he zeroed in on his specialization from his PhD in clinical psychology as well as forensic psychology from what is now Alliant International University. He founded a successful practice in Southern California that has led him to serve countless people with the focus of *engaging addiction*. What both Dr. Flores and Dr. Fick offered was not ivory-tower theory, but practical insights that any Christian may apply while seeking to engage those for whom Jesus died and rose, and who also battle addiction.[193]

While I interviewed Dr. Flores and Dr. Fick on different occasions, the following is presented as if the interviews were synchronized:

Easy to Feel Afraid to Try

> **Dr. Espinosa:** Gentlemen, I have the impression that the prospect of engaging someone with an addiction is intimidating for the average Christian. Why might this be the case?
>
> **Dr. Fick:** Attempting to help someone who battles addiction can be perplexing and often fraught with disappointment. The sense of ineptness may be because the assistance is often responded to with rejection. Both those offering assistance

---

[193] Roberto Flores de Apodaca, interview by author, Costa Mesa, California, February 20, 2020; Paul Fick, interview by author, Laguna Niguel, California, December 26, 2019, and January 28, 2020.

and the addict feel that it is insurmountable, especially in light of past failed attempts.

Dr. Flores: Assuming we're talking about the person who isn't at the stage when they're really impaired, it is kind of overwhelming; a very powerful force. It is governing them, and they can't handle it, so we are frightened by people not under control. Many therapists will say, "If you're addicted, I can't help you."

Satan's modus operandi is to lead people into isolation. Sin, the world, and the enemy want Christians to be afraid of the prospect of engaging addicts so that the addict will remain in isolation. Being aware of this, God's people must counter destructive isolation while being mindful that the Gospel is *for all people*.

Hard to Recognize Sometimes

Dr. Espinosa: Ok, how *difficult* is it for us to recognize some addictions, like food and sex?

Dr. Fick: The primary reason [for difficulty in recognition] is that sexual drive and hunger are innate elements of one's being. So, the concept of developing "healthy" behavior including moderation surrounding sexuality or food differs from seeking abstinence and sustained recovery with alcohol or drugs.

Dr. Flores: They are so ubiquitous, food especially because you can't do without it; and sex is extremely pleasurable and [for the most part] legal, so you can distract yourself pretty effectively. They are inherently positive. You need food and need sex. There is nothing ungodly about the sexual instinct. You can say you don't really need marijuana or alcohol.

Dr. Espinosa: So, let's assume we are clear about the ubiquitous nature of addiction. It is another thing, however, to get past the lying. If someone is going to lie to you, can we really be effective?

Dr. Fick: So much addiction is predicated on an intimacy deficit. So, if you already lack a capacity to connect intimately, and indeed greatly fear it, it is easier to lie than to be honest. Honesty requires intimacy.

Dr. Flores: [It is easy for them to lie] because they are so ashamed of themselves. They have a ruthless inventory of moral failings . . . so that's their currency: self-deceit, deceit of others.

Dr. Espinosa: What if someone flat out says, "If they're going to lie, then what's the point in trying to help?"

Dr. Fick: If you are going to try to help addicts who are honest, you are going to wind up helping no one. Do your best to come from compassion and the understanding that the lying is from (1) the desire to continue the addictive behavior . . . and (2) the truth is humiliating and scary. To try to help someone battling addiction, you will be tested in many ways, including your patience.

Dr. Flores: Well, geez, you're sinless?! . . . Recognize your shortcomings, and then you'll be more apt to realize what a privilege it would be to help someone, what an honor! If they allow you, it is a blessing . . . . See the lie like a little kid lies to you . . . realize they are lying to you because they are ashamed. Don't take it personally. This is not an affront to you. Don't be acrimonious. If they could do better, they would—so help them to do better.

What's Really Going On?

Dr. Espinosa: I've heard descriptors from you—Dr. Fick and Dr. Flores—that the addict will feel the truth is "humiliating

and scary," and that they lie "because they are ashamed."
What's really going on inside?

Dr. Fick: Most people struggling with addiction battle shame.
For many, that shame formed as a child, perhaps the result of
being a victim of childhood maltreatment. A very large Kaiser
study demonstrated the strong correlation between "Adverse
Childhood Experiences" (ACES) and the propensity for physiological, psychological, and behavioral difficulties including
addiction as an adult. Another core issue that is prevalent,
particularly with sexual issues, is a profound intimacy deficit. The fear of being intimately involved with others, and
I mean emotionally rather than sexually, is powerful. This
is one of the reasons I have great concern about children or
adolescents that overuse electronics to the exclusion of learning how to interact and be intimate with others face-to-face.

In addition to the core issues that spring from childhood experiences, most addicts feel tremendous shame about what they
have done. Usually, addiction comes with a very messy history that the addict is not proud of. When they enter recovery,
they are ashamed of what they have done, the lies they have
told, the people they have injured, et cetera.

We should admit to people—if we are given the opportunity
to gain trust—that we, too, have failed in many ways and that
it is only by the grace of God that we are able to go forward.

Dr. Flores: In the prison population, what they seem to lack is
meaning and purpose. This leads to loneliness. What makes
the difference in lives is when we get to be servants. The lonely
only think about consuming.

Each case is unique—sui generis—and there are infinite path-
ways. But what they seem to have in common . . . is that they
learn this and descend into it by alienation, ultimately from
God. But before being alienated from God, you get alienated

from loved ones. They grow up alienated, angry, and wounded. And very few are religious, maybe 5 percent. Most criminals are not psychopaths, hardened, but . . . lost souls without a connectedness to God, connectedness to Christ. They are adrift and on their own. So, if they can get temporary reprieve by using meth, they are willing to pay the price.

When to Share the Gospel

Dr. Espinosa: What's wrong with avoiding engaging with the Gospel "until the person gets past the addiction"?

Dr. Fick: The first thing that comes to mind is that there is a potential loss of opportunity to tell someone about Christ's love for them. But even more so, I think that choosing to delay such discussions is borne out of a lack of reliance on the work of the Holy Spirit. It is relying upon a presumption—often erroneous—that we know the "right" time to share the Word. Another rationale not to avoid such discussions is that "getting past the addiction" can be an exceedingly lengthy process filled with lapses and relapses. And, while it is not pleasant to talk about, not everyone in the process of "getting past the addiction" survives. Death is a reality of addiction. Finally, God's Word is healing, and addicts need this healing just as the rest of us sinners do.

Dr. Flores: It is a question of timing. . . . When is the person available and when do they have detox? That's when they are feeling so ashamed and vanquished; hopeless and helpless. Shortly after this may be the perfect time. When people are at their nadir, bottomed out, completely vanquished.

What Not To Say

Dr. Espinosa: So, if the Christian gives it to God and goes forward to engage the addict, what are some things *not* to say?

Dr. Fick: It's easy for people to come off as being judgmental and condemning even by the look in their eyes or the way they shake their head.

I think it is wise not to speak out of frustration and anger. This is challenging, as, if you have a loved one who is an addict, there likely have been many hurtful experiences, disappointments, and harsh words that have occurred. So do your best to be aware of your own thoughts and feelings and speak about your concern rather than being condemning or recounting all the failures in the addict's history. Don't bother pointing out how they have broken prior promises. They are well aware of that, and you are only adding to their shame.

We should never say things like, "You can stop anytime you want to," or "Let me remind you how damaging this is," or "You're only hurting yourself . . . ," as if they didn't already know that. They do, and their shame is prevalent.

Dr. Flores: Anything that accentuates their shame; anything that convicts, and makes them feel hopeless, worthless.

When Might We Share the Law?

Dr. Espinosa: Is there ever a time when we might share the Law?

Dr. Fick: Understand that stating the Law is sometimes necessary, especially while reinforcing the need for healing. If, however, the person with an addiction hears condemnation, they will shut you out and stop listening. I think the greater point is that addiction is putting something ahead of God.

[Just be aware that] when they are not denying their addiction, addicts' inner thoughts include a lot of self-condemnation.

Dr. Flores: Not then and there.

I personally enjoyed the combination of answers here. Dr. Flores's answer is probably *most often applicable, as the person caught in addiction is overcome with shame.* At the same time, Dr. Fick's point is important: The Law isn't for pointing out the addiction itself, which would add condemnation. Rather, Law might be effective when the addict needs encouragement to pursue healing.

A Generous Helping of the Gospel

Dr. Espinosa: Okay, let's get to the goal of engagement: sharing the Gospel. Let's talk about that.

Dr. Fick: So speaking about their need for redemption is tricky on the one hand because they are already down on themselves and you don't want to "pile on" and, on the other hand, they may be open to that because it is in line with how they view themselves. Of course, the Gospel, the Good News, is what may be missing for them. Hearing that they are loved despite their sin ("while we were still sinners" [Romans 5:8]) and that the love and sacrifice of Christ leads to freedom and eternal salvation can offer the addict (and non-addicts) the peace that passes all understanding. We pray that the Holy Spirit will give us the right words for a person at a given time.

Dr. Flores: My wife, Lucy, who is an educator, tells me that students don't care what you know until they know you care. I think [most people struggling with addiction] first need a good helping of the Gospel.

The addicted person is terrified, and feels out of control and descent into oblivion . . . so they are so frightened and anxious, they will scurry at the first sign that they are being criticized.

The mere fact that the court orders [them] to a program instead of prison is already an expression of Gospel. It says, "You are redeemable! . . . We are going to extend mercy to you." . . . When it comes time to help those around us, the psychological approach alone is insufficient. We know that we need to bring in the spiritual first; we must realize that our lives are out of control so that we can break out of egotism. . . . There is something greater than me: God!

Dr. Fick: An effective image of Christ is Him hanging on the cross. This depicts the extent to which He took on the person's sin, and it also reflects the complete love of Christ for that person. The image of the resurrected Christ is also powerful. Addicts will relate to the idea of being "buried" as they feel utterly overwhelmed with addiction and coping with life. The concept of resurrection is uplifting for a host of reasons, including the hope it brings. It is a powerful image for one who is lacking hope. Jesus as the Good Shepherd seeking the lost is another wonderful image. God cares for us and seeks us out. Another image that comes to mind is Jesus as the Great Physician. Addicts intensely feel the need for healing.

Dr. Flores: We can present Christ as Wonderful Counselor [Isaiah 9:6]! Rely on His wisdom, not yours. You don't have to carry this burden and blame. It's not all on your shoulders. Matthew 11:28–29: "Come to Me, all who labor and are heavy laden, and I will give you rest. Take My yoke upon you, and learn from Me, for I am gentle and lowly in heart, and you will find rest for your souls."

Engagement Triangle Point 3: Place and Cultural Influence

If there was ever an arena for being cognizant of the spiritual forces behind the issue, then this is it. Step back and see what is really going on: regardless of the mitigating circumstances, people loved by God are so swallowed by shame that they are perfect candidates to join the stream of secularism:

1. *Individualism* is rampant as those battling addiction feel isolated and alone.

2. *Relativism* takes over as addictive behavior is justified and rationalized.

3. *Skepticism* is the habitual response as the addict easily begins to lose hope.

But those are the cultural symptoms; the devil has an overarching scheme. The Lord warns us still in His Word: "The thief comes only to steal and kill and destroy" (John 10:10). He shoots his "flaming darts" (Ephesians 6:16) to accuse—and to accuse so much that people will enter despair. What is left to do? People run to manipulate the brain's reward system, numbing themselves while Satan's wave of lies covers them: "You *must* do this, because of what you *are!*" "He is a liar and the father of lies" (John 8:44). Too often he convinces people that his lies are true.

At the same time, the culture might be perpetuating the problem. Dr. Flores pointed out to me that the new terminology has "elasticized the concept [of addiction]."[194] He explained: "The principle is one of dysfunction: does it interfere [with your life]?" When this transition was taking place from addiction to disorder, one of Dr. Flores's colleagues said, "We've just added 15 million more patients." "The changes," Dr. Flores explained, "have been revolutionary really."

Dr. Flores succinctly stated the reason for concern: "How far does interference need to go before *dysfunction*? Psychology has over-medicalized problems in the human condition." In addition, not only have definitions expanded, he explained, "but the number of disorders keeps growing, upwards of 450 disorders. . . . Back in the '50s for *DSM-1*, there were about fifty." Dr. Flores put the situation in

---

[194] Apodaca, interview.

perspective: "It's not that people are becoming more crazy, but we are borrowing from normalcy."

PLACE

● **CULTURE**
- Resist Dysfunction
& Sin as the Norm

How does this relate to the spiritual battle? Simply, there are increased reasons for accounting for what God's Word identifies as *sin*. For example, why would anyone treat "fits of anger" (Galatians 5:20) as *sin* when it is better diagnosed—as Dr. Flores pointed out—as a *manic episode*? Not only is the culture *borrowing from normalcy* to expand disorders, but it is *replacing sin*. And when sin no longer exists, who needs a Savior from it?

The person battling addiction knows the truth because they know their shame. No matter how many diagnoses a person might receive, and regardless of the number of *disorders* they battle, the sufferer is convinced that their *whole person* is accursed.

But when Jesus was dying on the cross, the heavenly Father turned away from His Son (Matthew 27:46; Mark 15:34). This seems a horrific, coldhearted reaction, but it was a great affirmation of God's love and mercy *for us*. How? Because the Father *accepted* the Son's vicarious or substitutive offering of Himself *for us*. God has already turned away from our sin and dealt with it when it was on Jesus. In other words, *Jesus became our accursed persons*. He became our curse (Galatians 3:13), and He bore our shameful sin (1 Peter 2:24). What is left for us? In a word: freedom.

CHAPTER 11 DISCUSSION GUIDE

ENGAGING ADDICTION

UNCOVER INFORMATION

1. A basic definition of *addiction* is something that
   _____ a person.

2. In what way did King Solomon warn about extremes?

3. According to the title of Timothy Keller's book, what three
   things are capable of being spiritual addictions?

4. People with disorders often live with extreme _____.

5. What does Dr. Flores teach us about the trend of the number of
   disorders over the decades?

DISCOVER MEANING

1. What was St. Paul saying in 1 Corinthians 6:12? What did he mean?

2. Even the healthy Christian without an addiction *per se* or demonic influence still has an ongoing and uninterrupted inner battle. What is this?

3. There is such a thing as an achievement addict. What does this mean?

4. What does it mean to engage with "a generous helping of the Gospel," especially through the images of Christ recommended by Dr. Fick and Dr. Flores?

5. What does it mean that expanded *disorders* are replacing *sin*? We can never lose sight of the great need being addressed in engagement with the Gospel.

EXPLORE IMPLICATIONS

1. If we all have a sinful flesh (and we do), what are we capable of?

2. What is wrong with bypassing the consideration of spiritual influences when considering how we engage with an addiction?

3. How does the story of Brandon and Chloe suggest the importance of receiving Word and Sacrament while wrapping these with prayer and spoken confession of sin and faith?

4. What are the implications of individualism, relativism, and skepticism upon addiction?

5. What does the heavenly Father forsaking Jesus on the cross imply about what God has done with our "whole person" curse (the basis for our shame)?

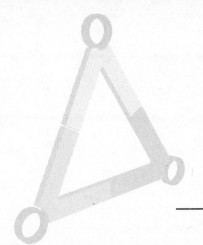

CHAPTER 12:
ENGAGING DEPRESSION

Engagement Triangle Point 1: Perspective and Approach

The etiology or causation of depression is not an attitudinal problem (though the attitude is impacted), nor should it ever be reduced to a mere sadness (though sadness often accompanies it). Depression is a disease that impacts the mind's ability to process stimuli, that is, the feedback of the world around the sufferer. The imbalance in the brain's neurotransmitters generates an alarming state of numbness. In the process, the person battling depression may feel out of control, desperate for some sense of normalcy, but this is elusive. For this reason, depression often leads to other problems like anxiety or alcohol addiction.

Exacerbating the situation is that because most people don't understand depression, things are said that tempt the person with depression to feel even more discouraged. "Why can't they just *snap out of it*?" And while this would be a terrible thing to say, well-meaning people say things like this all the time. That is, people with good intentions often give "advice" that just makes the problem worse. All the while, the person who is depressed can be filled with great shame and despair.

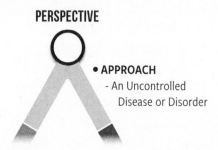

PERSPECTIVE

● APPROACH
- An Uncontrolled
  Disease or Disorder

For this reason, it is important to affirm the identity of the person battling depression so that the illness does not define them. That is, the engaging Christian will emphasize compassion, acknowledge their struggles, and remember that ministry is not about having all the answers, but about presence and love. In this way, depression's isolation is countered by the presence of God's ambassadors, those who confess Jesus.

On the spiritual plane, depression represents something for the devil to try to take advantage of. Depression is the opportunity for "false belief, despair, and other great shame and vice" (Small Catechism, Sixth Petition). Thus, we must pray against these attacks while a person experiences depression. For this reason, the Sixth Petition of the Lord's Prayer is especially applicable to the situation.

Small Catechism

The Sixth Petition: And lead us not into temptation.

What does this mean? God tempts no one. We pray in this petition that God would guard and keep us so that the devil, the world, and our sinful nature may not deceive us or mislead us into false belief, despair, and other great shame and vice. Although we are attacked by these things, we pray that we may finally overcome them and win the victory.

The Person Who Is Depressed Has Most Likely Already Been Visited by the Law

Most often, the person suffering depression is already fully convinced that they are helpless to make themselves whole. They are in an internal conflict that seems overwhelming. In effect, in these cases, the Lord has permitted the work of the Law that reveals terrible need long before the Christian comes to engage them with God's Word.

As serious as this is, however, the Christian may go straight to the Gospel in their engagement. The suffering one is already convicted and needy. And these, of course, are the ones for whom Christ came. The Gospel does not depend on feelings or relative health. Rather, the Gospel of God's free grace in His Son, Jesus Christ, goes to what the person with depression needs more than anything: unconditional love and mercy from God.

God's Special Revelation Related to Depression

While the word *depression* is not in God's Word, there are many scriptural references to situations and states of mind that are reminiscent of depression, at least to the extent that some of the possible symptoms of depression are described. And while we cannot make a one-for-one correspondence of these descriptions to say that they *are* symptoms of actual depression, the basic human experience associated with depression is no rarity in Scripture.

It is hard to imagine, for example, the extent of Job's misery. To say he entered a dysfunctional state of mind overflowing with pessimism and self-condemnation would not be an overstatement. While we are aware that he was also suffering from substantial physical ailments (see Job 2:7), we are also privy to his internal strife. What sort of condition of the soul would be represented if one was on the receiving end of one's own spouse saying what Job's wife said? She said to Job, "Do you still hold fast your integrity? Curse God and die" (Job 2:9). Perhaps it is *only* the depressed person who comes close to relating to Job.

The Sons of Korah in Psalm 42 examined the soul, however, and expressed their recognition that something was terribly wrong. They cried, "Why are you cast down, O my soul, and why are you in turmoil within me? Hope in God; for I shall again praise Him, my salvation and my God" (Psalm 42:5–6). What depressed person cannot relate to being "cast down," and who would deny that "turmoil" might be one of the better ways for describing the chaos within?

Such experiences were also known by the holy prophets of God. Jeremiah is case in point. He had the unenviable task of warning the Kingdom of Judah of the coming judgment, and then, of course, it was he who described the horrific scene of Jerusalem's destruction. Jeremiah wrote clearly and painfully, "My joy is gone; grief is upon me; my heart is sick within me" (Jeremiah 8:18). The extent of his agony was so great that he shockingly expressed, "Cursed be the day on which I was born" (Jeremiah 20:14)!

But if Jeremiah is indeed an example of what depression feels like, then we must go further to remind ourselves that he also knew the inestimable comfort of the Gospel. After the unspeakable calamity of Jerusalem's terrifying destruction, it was this same "weeping prophet"—as Jeremiah is also known—who spoke some of the most consoling words in all of Scripture: "For the Lord will not cast off forever, but, though He cause grief, He will have compassion according to the abundance of His steadfast love" (Lamentations 3:31–32).

Jeremiah was able to express this not because of the sway of emotions, but by the Holy Spirit leading him through faith in the promises of God's Word. He held to how the Lord looked upon him through the storms of life. He held to what God had promised in His steadfast love. This, too, the person who is depressed can do. After all, the Lord does not want anyone to be bound to the chains that flow from sin in the world, but rather to know the certain hope that on account of Christ, we know God as our heavenly Father, who loves us no matter what we go through in life. St. Paul wrote about this: "For you did not receive the spirit of slavery to fall back into fear, but you have received the Spirit of adoption as sons, by whom we cry, 'Abba! Father!'" (Romans 8:15).

The Record of One Who Has Gone Through It in Today's Culture

An incredibly poignant description of depression comes from Tracy Thompson, a finalist for a Pulitzer Prize for investigative reporting through her chronicle about her battle with depression.[195] Early in her book, her description of the disease is engrossing, and the way she personifies depression brings us closer to its insidious effects:

> My body aches intermittently, in waves, as if I had malaria.
> I eat with no appetite, simply because the taste of food is one
> of my dwindling number of pleasures. I am tired, so tired.
> Last night I lay like a pile of old clothes, and when [my hus-
> band] came to bed, I did not stir. Sex is a foreign notion. At
> work today I am forgetful; I have trouble forming sentences,
> I lose track of them halfway through, and my words keep
> getting tangled. I look at my list of things to do today, and
> keep on looking at it; nothing seems to be happening. Things
> seem sad to me . . . I call [depression] "Beast" because it suits
> him—though I imagine "him" not as a creature but as a force,
> something that has slipped outside the bounds of natural exis-
> tence, a psychic freight train of roaring despair.[196]

Tracy would probably say that she was not writing from a Christian worldview, but her description from a left-hand kingdom (civil realm) perspective is spot-on. She traces the origins of *depression* going back to the Greeks in the time of Hippocrates, who "described a mental condition involving prolonged and inexplicable feelings of fear and anxiety."[197] The Greeks traced this to an excess of "black bile" and thus the occasion for the term *melaena chole* was born. This is where we get our English word *melancholy*.[198]

Ms. Thompson writes, "Depression robs the mind of its normal power to concentrate and analyze."[199] Other symptoms inevitably follow:

---

[195] Tracy Thompson, *The Beast: A Reckoning with Depression* (New York: G. P. Putnam's Sons, 1995). Copyright © by Tracy Thompson. Reprinted by permission of Beth Vesel Literary Agency.

[196] Thompson, *The Beast*, 3-4.

[197] Thompson, *The Beast*, 9.

[198] Thompson, *The Beast*, 9.

[199] Thompson, *The Beast*, 11.

My emotions—my life—seemed out of control. Slowly, in ways invisible to me at the time, the depression was altering my personality. . . . The changes were not the symptoms of depression but coping mechanisms for dealing with it, and they built on existing personality traits. I had always been anxious to win others' approval, but now that need became insatiable; I had always been capable of charm, but now charm became a naked willingness to manipulate others to get what I wanted.[200]

But imagine that the person who is depressed is also totally unaware of the changes in their brain taking place.[201] In addition to being oblivious to changes in the brain, there is also a loss of feeling.[202] Furthermore, yet another dynamic takes place: Because the person battling depression is trying to find a framework for the ability to function and cope, "[they] cling to the very perceptions that are most distorted."[203] This distortion includes absolutist thinking: "I will be alone forever," or "This pain will never end."[204]

In all of this, there is fundamental shame forming in the heart and soul. They feel to blame for their condition. Tracy states that this "self-laceration was typical depressive behavior."[205] Here, God surprises us that those very people who seem to suffer most are in some important ways most especially blessed in their disposition for receiving the saving Gospel. Why should this surprise us? The Lord spoke: "Those who are well have no need of a physician, but those who are sick" (Matthew 9:12).

To be sure, depression is a kind of disease, an illness.[206] Tracy calls it "a chemical abnormality that [produces] *behavior*."[207] She elaborates:

---

200   Thompson, *The Beast*, 58.

201   Thompson, *The Beast*, 112.

202   Thompson, *The Beast*, 112.

203   Thompson, *The Beast*, 145-46.

204   Thompson, *The Beast*, 146.

205   Thompson, *The Beast*, 179.

206   Thompson, *The Beast*, 189.

207   Thompson, *The Beast*, 192.

"The expression 'My mind was going in circles' might be not simply a metaphor. . . . If you didn't have enough neurotransmitters in your brain, the electrical impulses they were supposed to ferry could simply wander around in circles for lack of everywhere else to go, or they could get lost. So the depressed person would obsess about things, or forget them."[208]

American Psychiatric Association Says This Is Real

If the reader has not experienced depression, then Ms. Thompson's descriptions might seem exaggerated. They're not. The American Psychiatric Association lists nine symptoms of Major Depressive Disorder. To know these is to be confronted by a living nightmare, and if this does not move the Christian to have immense compassion, then they should not bother with biblical engagement for the depressed.

1. Depressed mood most of the day, nearly every day, as indicated by either subjective report (e.g., feels sad, empty, or hopeless) or observation made by others (e.g., appears tearful).

2. Markedly diminished interest or pleasure in all, or almost all, activities most of the day, nearly every day (as indicated by subjective account or observation).

3. Significant weight loss when not dieting or weight gain (e.g., change of more than 5 percent of body weight in a month), or decrease in appetite nearly every day.

4. Insomnia or hypersomnia nearly every day.

5. Psychomotor agitation or retardation nearly every day (observable by others, not merely subjective feelings of restlessness or being slowed down).

6. Fatigue or loss of energy nearly every day.

---

[208] Thompson, *The Beast*, 219.

7. Feelings of worthlessness or excessive or inappropriate guilt (which may be delusional) nearly every day (not merely self-reproach or guilt about being sick).

8. Diminished ability to think or concentrate, or indecisiveness, nearly every day (either by subjective account or as observed by others).

9. Recurrent thoughts of death (not just fear of dying), recurrent suicidal ideation without a specific plan, or a suicide attempt or a specific plan for committing suicide.[209]

These are real issues when it comes to living with depression. And when the Christian is equipped with this proper **perspective** launching the engagement triangle, then there is truly an appropriate **approach** to be had. Many would say that given these complexities the Christian should bypass anyone who truly seems depressed. And this would be the wrong conclusion. Instead—and even in the face of substantive suffering—those who are depressed have a special place in the heart of God. Christians are called to love and to reach out in dedicated engagement, which testifies against the devil's attack through depression. These are not alone. These are not untouchables. These are ones for whom Jesus lived, died, and rose. These we will love, and these we will engage.

Engagement Triangle Point 2: People and Attitude

Dr. Shannon Gallina, PhD in clinical psychology (Alliant University, San Diego, California), has practiced as a clinical psychologist for twenty-five years with specializations in anxiety and depression. More was needed in the way of connecting with people who are depressed. How can we bridge the gap? How can we find common ground? How do we come alongside people immersed in depression? Dr. Gallina was immensely helpful.[210] Our interview began:

---

[209] *DSM-5*, 160–61.
[210] Shannon Gallina, interview by author, Mission Viejo, CA, October 4, 2019.

Dr. Espinosa: Dr. Gallina, how would you define *depression*?

Dr. Gallina: Depression can be situational (caused by a more-or-less identifiable external event or situation), a chemical imbalance, or a more diffuse cause as anger turned inward toward the self. Depression, despite its cause, presents in a combination of symptoms and signs. For example, depressed mood, decreased or increased appetite, weight gain or loss, insomnia or hypersomnia, excessive or inappropriate guilt, isolation and withdrawal, loss of enjoyment in activities that used to be fun, tearfulness, hopelessness, preoccupation with death or dying, to name a few. There are gradations and levels so that severity can be mild, moderate, or severe.

While these "symptoms and signs" were myriad, it is nevertheless astounding that so many people just assume depression is a bad case of sadness. Such an assumption implies a simple solution: "just be more positive" (or something to this effect). Would Dr. Gallina maintain a distinction between depression and "having the blues"?

Dr. Espinosa: Thank you, doctor. I think some people assume that depression is simply sadness. Is it?

Dr. Gallina: No, it isn't, and while apparent sadness may accompany depression, it takes time in therapy to determine whether it's one or the other.

So, there it was: depression cannot be reduced to sadness, and I was about to find out just how additionally complex it can be. Our interview continued.

Dr. Espinosa: Are there *accompanying* disorders?

Dr. Gallina: Absolutely. Depression often leads to anxiety or anxiety can lead to depression. Sometimes it can be difficult to know which came first, so these two are frequently combined. So, in addition to the depressive symptoms, anxiety brings a heightened arousal and overreaction to stimuli and makes a difference in concentration and sleep, producing racing thoughts, physiological changes in the heart and in breathing. Fear—general or specific—is heightened, and this leads to startled responses and general unease.

When one backs up and takes inventory of the flood of symptoms indicating what must be an exhausting effort to cope, it is no wonder that so many people who are depressed can become institutionalized. I wondered if depression was on the rise.

> **Dr. Espinosa:** Dr. Gallina, I feel as though we hear a lot about depression in the culture. Am I imagining things?

> **Dr. Gallina:** Well, it's *prevalent* in our culture. Causation has a lot to do with the world we live in and the demands we place on ourselves . . . through social media, education, and careers. I have many clients who come to me with symptoms of depression and it is notable how many of them say to me, "I know it's not a 'real' problem, it's just a first-world [minor] problem." I think this is a statement of how our culture specifically translates to *symptoms* of depression for some people, and that often the individuals suffering depression perceive the causes of their depression as issues that should not cause significant distress. Some examples of external situations contributing to depression that my clients describe as first-world problems are feeling "behind" in career or social activities compared to their peers on social media, becoming preoccupied [for example] with the number of "followers" they have in their social media posts.

As a pastor-theologian, I was intrigued by what Dr. Gallina just spelled out. God warns us about our entanglements with the world (1 John 2:15–17). She had just described how the culture itself can contribute to the formation of depression, which is to say that I was discovering that depression ought not be reduced to a matter of *either* nature *or* nurture, but rather may accurately be understood as a combination of the two.

> **Dr. Espinosa:** So, the causes of depression can possibly be attributed to the way we live?

> **Dr. Gallina:** I think so. In many respects, we are just spread too thin.

For myself, I felt as though Dr. Gallina was describing our way of connecting: if we understand the background, then the Christian can relate to the negative influences of the world, to say nothing of the insidious and deceiving nature of sin itself. But I needed to turn a corner and zero in on engagement.

> **Dr. Espinosa:** So, our concern in the engagement triangle is how Christians engage. How might we engage someone impacted by depression?

> **Dr. Gallina:** If a person seems as though they have a depressed mood, don't be afraid to ask open-ended questions like, "Tell me what's going on" or "You seem sad; I want to hear about it." Realize that anyone struggling with depression is naturally folding in on themselves. So be persistent, but gentle. Just keep in mind that because of guilt and the fear of being judged, they often feel like it's hard to connect and express. So, help them get into it. Let them know that you *want* to understand (not that you *do* understand). Validate them and ask them questions like, "Tell me what it's like for you." It needs to be mentioned in any discussion about depression that suicidal intention must always be assessed. The professionals are qualified to do this assessment, but in my opinion, after an initial inquiry about a person's signs and symptoms of depression, the gentle, compassionate yet direct question

about the presence of suicidal ideation must happen. "Because I care about you, I want you to be safe and need to ask if you are having thoughts of wanting to die." Asking this question does not "put the idea in their head," but it can help save a life.

Dr. Espinosa: Dr. Gallina, what if the person confirms they are suicidal? We are talking about *laypeople* engaging here, not trained psychologists. What should the Christian do if this is the case?

Dr. Gallina: If the person you're engaging is suicidal, then do the following:

1. Validate their courage for telling you this. Show compassion.

2. Stay with them and call the National Suicide Prevention Lifeline (NSPL) at 800-273-8255, or 911, or go to a hospital emergency room.

3. Stay with them until help arrives, or if intervention can wait a day or more, make an appointment with a mental health professional, then verify by following up between parties. In this case, you can call National Alliance on Mental Illness (NAMI) at 800-950-6264, that's 800-950-NAMI.[211]

Dr. Gallina was strong on this point that suicidal intention must be assessed as much as possible, and she was helpful in offering a straightforward plan on how to serve anyone considering taking their life. This one point by itself might make a Christian avoid engagement with people who are depressed: "It's just too much responsibility!" But I think that while Dr. Gallina was bold to say it, she was also confident that God leads His people to care enough to ask the tough questions whenever the Lord permits engagement. This is not being nosy. It is being loving. But imagine: if anyone permits this level of openness,

---

[211] Both interviewees Dr. Shannon Gallina and Rev. Todd Peperkorn, with the contribution of Elizabeth Snyder (MA in clinical psychology, Rosemead School of Psychology, La Mirada, CA), and myself devised this plan.

then it is a sign that God has opened a wide door so that the Gospel might be powerfully received. Nevertheless, I could imagine what some Christians might be thinking at this point.

> **Dr. Espinosa:** Dr. Gallina, these seem like personal questions. Is this too much too soon?
>
> **Dr. Gallina:** A depressed person feels isolated, as if nobody understands, so if they see that someone is sincere about wanting to listen, this goes a long way. These questions show the person we care enough to ask the uncomfortable questions and hear the uncomfortable answers. This is love in action. Validation is important. In these instances, people don't feel lovable and often, it boils down to God. That is, someone who is depressed can also feel as though they are not good enough for God.

I loved it. Dr. Gallina did not hold back on the fact that this boldness was a matter of "love in action" as she put it. She was speaking the language of Christians truly representing God. If the Christian steps out this way, then God's love can seem real. Still, I wanted to know more on the specifics.

> **Dr. Espinosa:** This sounds as though if we are going to step out and engage someone showing signs of depression that we really need to be considerate about what we say and what we should not say. True?
>
> **Dr. Gallina:** That's right. Never say, "I know how you feel," because we don't; and don't trivialize things by saying something like, "You should get more sun . . . Vitamin D helps," or "You should try x, y, z; my friend had depression and it helped her," or "You're fine, you'll get over this," or "You're not depressed, you'll get over it in time."

Dr. Espinosa: Okay, so don't assume to understand and don't trivialize. What are we aiming for then?

Dr. Gallina: To address the fact that for someone who is battling depression, it's important to realize that often, deep down, they feel as though they're not lovable and not good enough. There is no convincing with rationality that one is good enough and lovable. Bottom line: faith is the answer. They need to hear, "God loves you." This is where a person gets their value. Often the way they see themselves stems all the way back to their childhood, and along the way, they became convinced that they are not lovable or valuable. So, focus on God's love instead of trying to convince someone to feel worthy; let them know that they are already loved through Jesus Christ. And when we share this message, we do it with compassion, kindness, empathy, attentiveness, and unconditional positive regard.

Dr. Gallina had brought it home for us, so to speak. There it was, the bottom line: "faith is the answer," "focus on God's love," and "let them know that they are already loved through Jesus Christ." And then there was this amazing phrase: "unconditional positive regard." Wasn't this the way God through His Son looked and looks upon us? This was key for engaging anyone who might be depressed.

Unconditional Positive Regard

In some ways, imagining engaging someone with depression can seem very intimidating. But Dr. Gallina had inspired a summary that sees the forest through the trees and makes the prospect of engaging under these circumstances realistic and doable. These points serve as a basic guide and describe *unconditional positive regard*:

1. People who are depressed can be highly receptive to engagement to hear the Gospel, so begin by showing you're willing to listen, as this goes a long way.

2. Validate both the existence of the disease *and* God's unconditional love by being gentle, not claiming to understand but showing that you *want* to understand.

3. Step out and ask open-ended questions or request, *"Tell me what it's like for you."*

4. With compassion, don't be afraid to ask the person if they are having any thoughts about wanting to die. Let them see how much you care. If they say yes, then use the simple three-step intervention listed above.

5. Tell them, *"God loves you."* Then share Christ, whose love and mercy covers the strong feelings that they are not lovable nor valuable. *"In Christ, you're already loved, and in Christ, you're inestimably valuable to God!"*

Don't Make It Complicated

These engagement insights help us connect to the second point of the engagement triangle: **people**. And as you might recall from chapter 5, this is all about getting into the shoes—as much as we possibly can—of the other person. This is our engagement **attitude**. It isn't rocket science, and it flows from the unconditional positive regard Dr. Gallina was describing. Our whole attitude toward the person who is depressed is that in the face of their feeling unlovable and invaluable, they are absolutely loved and infinitely valued by God in Christ. So, the first step is to just be genuine in caring. Ask the basic questions other people are too afraid to ask and show that the person is important by taking an interest.

PEOPLE

- **ATTITUDE**
  - Don't Try to Fix, but Offer
    Unconditional Positive Regard

More Important to Listen Than to Try to Fix

At the same time, we cannot underestimate that it can still feel intimidating to engage someone who is depressed. I wanted a pastor's guidance on all of this—but not just any pastor. I needed to speak to a pastor who was not only outstanding in the faithful proclamation of the Word of Christ and in the right administration of the Holy Sacraments, but who also has experienced depression. The Lord led me to the pastor I needed. I was blessed to sit down with Rev. Todd Peperkorn, pastor of Holy Cross Lutheran Church in Rocklin, California, doctoral candidate at the Aquinas Institute of Theology in St. Louis, Missouri, and author of the book *I Trust When Dark My Road: A Lutheran View of Depression* (Lutheran World Relief and Human Care, 2009).[212]

> **Pastor Espinosa:** Reverend Peperkorn, what should we be considerate of when speaking to a person with depression?
>
> **Pastor Peperkorn:** I would start with that it is much more important to listen than to try and fix. With almost certainty, whatever you think [might be the problem] is something they have obsessed about for years. Don't say things like, "Get more sunlight." We need to be aware that with the googlization of health, everyone can be an expert and know nothing. Often what you hear is [baloney]. On the spiritual end, the most

---

[212] Todd Peperkorn, interview by author, Rocklin, California, January 28, 2020.

228

common answer is "Well, if you just had more faith, you would be totally normal." [Many popular teachers in the pop-culture church] across the board say, "If you had more faith, if you made better decisions, then you would not suffer from mental illness."

Pastor Espinosa: Pastor, what do you think about this idea that faith should eliminate mental illness?

Pastor Peperkorn: It's an irrational conclusion. You would never say this to someone with a broken leg. This trend began with the premise that there is no such thing as mental health, only physiological problems and demonic possession. What is "mental" is from hidden, unconfessed sin. So, "counseling" [as it was viewed by many in pop-culture Christianity] is to exhort depressed people to live better. This defined "counseling" in seminaries for years. Added to this model was pop psychology—positive thinking [baloney]—everything is good and positive, and this is driven by a prosperity gospel.[213] Any modern take about depression was shaped by this mentality.

Pastor Espinosa: Are such ideas still the status quo in the church?

Pastor Peperkorn: Things started to crack around the time Rick Warren's son committed suicide in 2013 and Rick said, "I wonder if something else is going on here." If we can learn how to walk alongside someone, not pretend that we have the answers to all their problems, recognize that they're suffering, that it does suck, and I can't wave a wand, then we have something to offer. But the number one thing is the simple acknowledgment that something *is* going on and that it sucks, and then doors will be open to be able to care for this person.

---

[213] The "prosperity gospel" leads one to claim that God pours out earthly blessings upon those with sufficient faith in His "kingdom" promises. Since Christ rules all things, Christians should claim and expect to be blessed in every way, including financial windfalls, beaming physical health, and comfortable life circumstances. Being spared depression would be taken for granted.

This reminded me of what Dr. Gallina had said about the importance of *validation*. *By simply acknowledging what is painful and unpleasant, the person who is depressed can know that they are not talking to an arm-chair psychologist trying to fix them, but someone who says, "I believe you and I know this is real."* I was gearing up for my next question and didn't realize I was about to hear what would establish an important truth: for many if not most people living with depression, God's Law had already visited them through life experience. They were already fully cognizant of their desperate need for help. It was now left for the Christian to engage with the Gospel. In addition, Pastor Peperkorn provided one of the most vivid descriptions of *what depression feels like* that I had ever heard. I realized as I listened to him that Christians—equipped with this understanding—can finally be in a position to be filled with compassion when speaking to one for whom Jesus died who has depression.

Pastor Espinosa: Pastor Peperkorn, what makes such people unique?

Pastor Peperkorn: They live under the Law in a way that few people experience. This is like you don't have to preach Law at a funeral because the Law is in the casket. For those who are depressed, the Law is continually present in their mind. Whether the cause is spiritual or physiological or situational, you know there are dozens of causes for what we would put under the umbrella of depression. It is the living embodiment of *incurvatus in se*[214] because what you are talking about is the ability of your body to process input. Because of the dopamine regulation, your body does not process stimulus as it is supposed to. It is almost like a parallel to insulin resistance. Your body is not processing as it should so that some things are over-processed and other things under-processed. It's like everything is turned sideways. What that means is that the solution is to cut off stimulants, to cut off the inputs. This is

---

[214] See chapter 2 under the subtitle, "Knowing the Severity of People's Spiritual Problem."

why people with mental illness typically self-isolate—because that stimulus might be sight, sound; it could be noise, crowds, or anything that is going to provide stimulus that's a kind of overload to the system. This is like your computer running too many processes at the same time and it gets stuck. This is your brain on depression. It's the inability to process, and it's not necessarily sadness. Sometimes for women, it might be a kind of emotionalism [manifest by] constant crying ... easily set off. For men, it often comes out as anger and irritability. All this just shows how the person is unable to process all the stuff coming at them, and it's just right there and this is how you deal with it. So, it's like all the stimulation is coming in wrong, and my way of interpreting is doing the same.

Pastor Espinosa: What can be done about this over-stimulation cycle?

Pastor Peperkorn: The way to simplify is to simply stop the stimulus, to isolate. But, one of the great ironies of this whole thing is that every lick of research says that people are healthier in communities. But you know, it's kind of "duh"; it's not rocket science: mental health can be positively impacted by community and specifically the church.

Pastor Espinosa: It's exciting to think that our one-to-one personal engagement might be God's way of connecting someone to the Body of Christ. This is all the more reason why we need to approach engagement with the person who is depressed very carefully. Take us back to how we do this.

Pastor Peperkorn: So, we need to think in terms of non-judgment, listening more than speaking, caring for people on their own terms. And maybe I can't care for this person directly. It might be that I can care for one of their family members, who may very well be suffering as much as the one with the disease. I mean—speaking for myself—as a husband, as a father, and also as a pastor, you know, you can argue with me, cuss me out, fight and do whatever, and that's kind of water off my back. But if you say something or do something to my family, I'm going after you. You know what I'm thinking about here. And in the same way, if you do something nice for my family, I am yours for life. And again, this is what the church does: it cares for people in need. But it's hard because it's time-consuming and really hard and there is no answer we can give or it may not work, et cetera. [there are many excuses not to engage and seek to serve]. But we're not talking about fixing. We are simply talking about establishing a relationship. That means the illness does not define them.

Pastor Peperkorn had just landed a crucial insight: *"the illness does not define them."* Engagement learns not to objectize people. The concern is to love people because they *are* people with the *universal* sin problem, but extended God's *universal* grace solution in Christ. But how does the Christian show others that they really know this and believe this? The Christian will validate the truth: *the illness does not define the person who is depressed.* Still, I couldn't wait to hear Pastor's elaboration on this concept.

> **Pastor Espinosa:** I have a feeling I know exactly what you mean, but would you expand on what you mean by "the illness does not define them"?

> **Pastor Peperkorn:** There are many things people allow themselves to be identified by rather than being identified by their Baptism, their identity in Christ. I know a diabetic who doesn't really like being called a diabetic, because it makes it sound like *he* is the disease. You wouldn't call somebody a "depressoretic" or a heart "attackeric" or whatever. How we speak about people kind of shows how we value them and how we define them. Use people's names and don't allow labels to define them. Address people as human beings and not as a sin, and that's kind of the underlining thing: if you allow a

sin to define a person, well, guess what? You've kind of lost the conversation before you've even begun.

Sometimes the Common Ground Is "I Have No Idea What You're Going Through"

Pastor Espinosa: Pastor Peperkorn, what are things we should *avoid* saying?

Pastor Peperkorn: Good question. "I know how you feel," but you may not. There is a fine line, I think, between sympathy and a desire to have sympathy for someone and belittling that person's situation. That is, that could be very delicate, be very tricky. I want to have sympathy with them. In a conversation, you are trying to find common ground. Sometimes the common ground might be, "I have no idea what you're going through. Tell me about it." And don't pretend like you know, because you were sad one day. Sure, "I know just what it's like to not be able to get out of bed for six months." You don't. So, recognizing limitations in your own experience actually allows you to enter into their experience.

Pastor Espinosa: That last quote was gold. Okay, what are some of the best things we could say?

Pastor Peperkorn: What can I do? How can I help? Or thinking about that sideways, is there anything I can do for your family or for somebody else? And again, I really believe very firmly that in that sideways angle of figuring out ways of showing mercy that probably won't fix things. It won't solve everything, but what they are going to get out of this is that they are being treated like a real person; that you have some understanding that something is not right; that you want to help and not patronize them.

When Engagement Seems to Stall,
Consider Offering a Prayer; Speak God's *Pro Nobis*

Pastor Espinosa: If we find that the person suffering from depression doesn't want the Gospel, that they don't want to hear about Christ, how do we respond?

Pastor Peperkorn: They most certainly will. I spent six months when I was on disability not being able to read, not being able to read anything, not even comic books because I couldn't process the information on the page. In the same way, it was nearly impossible for me to actually hear the Word of God or go to church because of what my mind was telling me all the time: all of those things are fine, but it's just not for me. It doesn't apply, because you know, *x, y, z*. Because of what kind of a person you are; because of what's going on. It's not rational. This is not a logical conversation, but chaos. I think the language of *disorder* [is appropriate] because that doesn't take much to bind it with sin. What is happening is that your life, your world, your brain is not ordered as God has intended. It's broken. Things don't fit as they are supposed to. So, sitting down and having a conversation with someone who has depression isn't going to follow the 1, 2, 3 [evangelism program] steps because you know it's all disordered. [The person who is depressed] needs order in the sense of regularity.

Pastor Espinosa: How do I as an individual Christian help bring order to the person who is depressed?

Pastor Peperkorn: It might be in conversation . . . and there is benefit in praying out loud with them. I use prayer as a way of giving voice to what they've said. This means that God is going to hear it because we are praying it. But they are also going to hear it so that they know we were actually listening. The fact that we acknowledge what is going on with them is huge. And we can pray to God that we have no idea what He is going to do with it, but that we are bringing it to the Lord so that we are not alone in this thing. Also, we can pray for or with family members. Prayer is the ultimate way, I think, of opening doors because it gives voice to what is happening. It might mean praying a psalm, you know. One of the psalms I use nearly every time I have a conversation with someone with mental illness or depression is Psalm 73 [v. 26]: "My flesh and my heart may fail, but God is the strength of my heart and my portion forever." That the Gospel is not about my heart being able to say or feel or act in a certain way, but that God is [my strength]. But there is also a danger here: the danger is to turn the Bible into "take two Bible passages, and call me in the morning," so that this is just another way of falling into legalism. So, I'm kind of circumspect to not pepper somebody with a lot of stuff because that is also going to make you sound like you are sort of using an atomic hammer trying to whack them with answers and hope that one of the answers stick. Using the Bible as a magical incantation, so that the right Bible verse will go *bing!* and every problem will be solved. That is not how the Scriptures are intended.

Pastor Espinosa: Pastor, are there any other resources we can offer someone while engaging them for Christ?

Pastor Peperkorn: What is missing in depression is the *pro nobis*, the "for you" character, because I don't believe that it is for me. It may be for everyone else, but somehow or another—and this seems irrational I know—it is not for me. So, look for opportunities to speak God's forgiveness in every possible place. Even in conversation, if someone is troubled by something, I would ask, "So, do you want to get rid of it?" Be ready to extend Christ's forgiveness right then and there. This is why I really like the language of *engagement*. That actually means being there, showing guts, and not pretending to have all the answers, but going in and trying.

Engagement Triangle Point 3: Place and Cultural Influence

Sin, the world, and the devil throw many curve balls when it comes to trying to get a grip on a basic and right view about depression. Two basic problems arise on account of negative cultural influence as we consider the third point on the engagement triangle: **place.**

1. Depression is just fashionable, and it's getting easier for people in the culture to isolate themselves anyway. For this reason, just live and let live. Here, the Christian is tempted to pretend nothing is really wrong and that there really isn't a good time to engage people who are depressed. Here the Gospel is indefinitely put off.

2. Depression is an ultimate scarlet letter and a frightening monster. The intricacies are so beyond us that one will feel instantaneously overwhelmed if engagement is permitted. The culture says, "Off limits!" and the demeanor of the depressed person says, "Stay away!" Here the Gospel is flippantly cut off.

PLACE

• **CULTURE**
- Resist Putting Off or
  Cutting Off the Gospel

These cultural inferences, however, are deceptions. There is nothing normal about the *dis*order of depression. While we should accept its reality and show compassion, we should resist the temptation to pretend that either nothing should be done, or that nothing can be done to help. Christ our Lord came for the sick, which includes all people. He did not hold back. He didn't allow us to drown in sin, nor did He treat us as lepers.

If you recall, we have been warning about the big three problems perpetuated in the culture: (1) individualism; (2) relativism; and (3) skepticism. We must be mindful that as Christians these things try to invade our minds and hearts toward those with depression. That is, these problems occur as a two-way street in relationship *not only within people who are depressed*, but also in the Christian *suddenly tempted to avoid all engagement.*

Individualism is the tendency for isolation (including detachment from the life-giving Word of Christ), and isolationism marks the one with depression. Here, a kind of individualism and preoccupation with the self is practically inevitable within the sufferer. However, individualism also strikes the Christian who reasons that engagement should be avoided. "It is just too much work to extend myself this way," so the sinful flesh says, and in this way, we permit our individualism to join the bandwagon of the end-times sign: "the love of many will grow cold" (Matthew 24:12).

Relativism is also an inherent problem with depression. Again, in the effort to desperately cope with the onslaught of something that is beyond the control of the one with depression, distorted perceptions become the norm. Inherently, therefore, depression produces a kind of relativism. But relativism also confronts the Christian who could engage with the Gospel. "Yes, God calls us to love our neighbor and to share the life-giving Gospel of Christ, but perhaps depression is somehow the exception to the rule. Maybe the chemical imbalance will render the Gospel ineffective, and maybe the loving thing to do is to honor the person who is trying to avoid overstimulation." This is when the Christian gives in to relativism. We can never predict when the Holy Spirit will choose to work through the Gospel, the power of God unto salvation. We should not be the ones to limit His work. Stick with what is true, trust in God, and treat the person with depression as a real person for whom the real Savior came.

Depression, of course, is also a breeding ground for skepticism. Tremendous self-blame and shame fill the mind and soul of the person living with depression. In such a condition, it is easy to feel skeptical toward any potential help. This is to be expected. What is less excusable is when the Christian permits skepticism to cut off the life-giving Gospel. "Can people entrenched in depression *really* be receptive to the Gospel? *Did God really say, 'all nations' [all people] should hear it?*" When these thoughts come, the sinful flesh must be crucified, the world's influence must be rejected, and Satan must be resisted so that he would flee from us (James 4:7).

CHAPTER 12 DISCUSSION GUIDE

ENGAGING DEPRESSION

UNCOVER INFORMATION

1. Is depression simply a problem with the attitude or mere sadness? Why or why not?

2. The person who is depressed has most likely already been visited by the _____. So, what should we emphasize immediately while engaging them?

3. How would you describe Tracy Thompson's descriptions of depression presented in this chapter?

4. What did Dr. Gallina say about how the way we live in our culture can contribute to forming depression?

5. In Pastor Peperkorn's first interview answer, he says that we should *not* try to do what?

DISCOVER MEANING

1. What does it mean that we not allow depression to define the person?

2. What do we mean that the Law has most likely already visited the person with depression?

3. Apply the significance of Matthew 9:12 to the person who is depressed.

4. What does Dr. Gallina mean when she says we should offer *validation* when we speak to the person who is depressed?

5. What's wrong with this idea: "If you had more faith, if you made better decisions, then you wouldn't be depressed"?

EXPLORE IMPLICATIONS

1. If depression leads to isolationism, what spiritual temptations and devilish accusations could develop?

2. If Jeremiah stated what he did as recorded at Jeremiah 8:18, what are *we* capable of?

3. The depressed person feels to blame for their condition, and as Tracy Thompson says, "self-laceration [is] typical depressive behavior." What does this mean for the way we engage someone who is depressed?

4. If we practice *unconditional positive regard*, what five things can flow from this? Please discuss the five points.

5. How can saying sincerely, "I have no idea what you're going through. Tell me about it," be so powerful for engagement with a person suffering with depression?

CONCLUSION

As we have considered the **engagement triangle**, there is little question that God's **perspective** about our **approach** is vital. We go forward putting Christ first, full of His love for people, and relying upon His Word. When Law is necessary, we stand ready to give it. And when the Law has done its work, we proceed with the saving Gospel. At the same time, before we say a word, we begin with our *own* hearts. First things first: God says we are to honor Christ in our hearts as holy (1 Peter 3:15).

PERSPECTIVE

With this in place, we proceed to "make a defense"—testify to the truth of the Gospel—giving an answer to the question, "Why do you hope as you do?" Why would anyone ever ask this question, or even intimate that it's on their mind? Because Christians have a chance to live differently.

The changing winds in the world do not dictate our peace. We know who always holds us. We see the bigger picture. So, we are ready to point people to the Savior, who forgives the sins of the world. But the

perspective and **approach** don't end there, as we are directed by the Holy Spirit to do this with gentleness toward those we engage with *and* with respect toward the Lord, who is always there with His people. That is, *engagement is among three, never just two.*

The second point of the engagement triangle is **people**. Here we have the opportunity to hone our **attitude** as we engage. How do we actually interact? St. Paul informs us of his strategy in 1 Corinthians 9:22: "I have become all things to all people, that by all means I might save some." *We strive to establish common ground.* When the common ground is realized, respect becomes genuine and trust begins to form.

PEOPLE

We must make the most of it so that the Holy Spirit might lead us to see the real connections we have with others. When Christians do this sincerely, they demonstrate that they do not engage with an agenda. They do not engage as they objectivize people. Christians engage because they love—knowing full well that God loved them first (1 John 4:19)—and love does not lead us to posture by being argumentative, but rather inspires us to seek with all our might to know how we stand *with* people, instead of standing *against* them.

The third point of the engagement triangle is **place**. We must consider the cultural impact upon us and upon those we engage. Everyone is influenced by the traditions, values, ideas, trends, and assumed "truths" of the culture. The challenges of individualism, relativism, and skepticism practically seep through our current milieu. *How will these things impact our engagement with those for whom Jesus lived, died, and rose to give them the Good News of the resultant forgiveness of sins, and the gift of eternal life with our Creator and Redeemer?*

PLACE

In addition, we mustn't forget that what influences our engagement is not simply what we observe empirically in the culture, but also what is invisible, as in "the cosmic powers over this present darkness" (Ephesians 6:12). All these bear upon our communicating face-to-face with another human being.

Engagement is not learning a "sales pitch," it is not trying to prove that the Bible is true, it is not trying to win an argument, and it is not the occasion for serving pride so that you can feel pious and holy in front of another person. It is not memorizing a long outline of illustrations, Scriptures, and talking points. It is, again, loving the person in front of you. Caring about them, taking an interest, giving them your full attention, and remembering that as you do these things God is with you. He cares about your effort because God loves the person you're talking to and wants them to be saved and come to the knowledge of the truth (1 Timothy 2:4).

We are helped by sticking with basic concepts: all people face things like guilt for wrongs (sins) committed, shame (sensing that there is something missing or wrong with themselves), fear in the face of death, and at least an inkling of being aware of the signs of chaos in our world. While all people know these things, not all people will admit to them, *but many if not most will.* When they do, we have opportunity to keep it simple and make it clear as Pastor Jasa taught us (see the Introduction):

1. Who did Jesus die for?

2. How many sins did He pay for?

3. Which one of your sins did Jesus forget to pay for?

We should remind ourselves that these things are *good news*. We are not condemning anyone. Much to the contrary, we are informing as to *how we know that God loves us*! Imagine that! We are called as God's royal priests to tell other people that they are loved by God! What a privilege!

Still, sometimes we are thrown some curveballs. Sometimes there is a pall that tries to block basic and simple engagement. In this current volume, we've considered some of the more common circumstances, and in each case, we have discussed how the engagement triangle applies to each one:

	PERSPECTIVE	PEOPLE	PLACE
SCIENCE	Faith and science integrated	Neither need absolute proof	Resist either-or
POLITICS	All three estates needed	All desire peace and freedom	Resist militant or silent
PERSONHOOD	Defend sanctity of all persons	Look past problem, see person	Resist secularism
SEXUALITY	God's order is the issue	Come alongside people	Resist distortion of love
ADDICTION	Causes great shame	Compassion reigns	Resist dysfunction as norm
DEPRESSION	Uncontrolled disorder	Don't try to fix; instead have positive regard	Resist putting off Gospel

The last thing we are doing in engagement is getting on a high horse. We don't become aware of these challenges to the faith listed above in order to judge people. If we do, then we've lost the biblical vision for engagement before we begin. Rather, we are engaging people just like us who have things that affect the way they see the world. We all have the same basic problem because we are all sinners and fall short of God's perfect will. So, we approach these things with great humility and remember that God has granted us the privilege to share His love.

The people who are enveloped in these issues—those who might advocate science to the extent that faith is rejected; those who live with political angst to breed hatred; those who disregard the life of anyone (weak, small, sick, elderly, alienated, or broken); those who live in confusion about God's order and His gift of male and female; those drenched in shame from the addictions that control them; or those overcome by the dark pit of depression that is beyond their ability to heal themselves—*these people* God loved so much that He gave up His Son, Jesus, to give each and every one life. These are no worse than the most holy Christian. These are loved every bit as much.

Who will have this vision and think it worthwhile to engage so that people would finally meet someone who does not approach them in order to condemn? Who will make themselves low enough to serve anyone they meet? Who will be as Christ to those who have never seen Him in a Christian before?

We are called to engage. It is God's will. It is God's command. It is what royal priests do. It is what Christians *get* to do! This **engagement triangle** is a way for us to also glorify God: Father, Son, and Holy Spirit. It is a way for us finally to live in faith that engages the culture.

BIBLIOGRAPHY

American Psychiatric Association. *Diagnostic and Statistical Manual of Mental Disorders: DSM-5*. 5th ed. Arlington, VA: American Psychiatric Association, 2013.

Bloom, John. "Science and Christianity." Lecture, Biola University, La Mirada, CA, Spring 2000.

Bork, Robert H. *Slouching towards Gomorrah: Modern Liberalism and American Decline*. New York: HarperCollins, 1996.

Bray, Gerald, ed. *1–2 Corinthians*. Ancient Christian Commentary on Scripture, New Testament VII. Downers Grove, IL: InterVarsity Press, 1999.

Bray, Gerald, ed. *James, 1–2 Peter, 1–3 John, Jude*. Ancient Christian Commentary on Scripture, New Testament XI. Downers Grove, IL: InterVarsity Press, 2000.

Bruce, F. F. *The Book of the Acts*. Rev. ed. The New International Commentary on the New Testament. Grand Rapids, MI: William B. Eerdmans, 1988.

Chemnitz, Martin, and Johann Gerhard. *The Doctrine of Man in Classical Lutheran Theology*. Edited by Herman A. Preus and Edmund Smits. Translated by Mario Colacci, Lowell Satre, J. A. O. Preus Jr., Otto Stahlke, and Bret H. Narveson. Minneapolis: Augsburg, 1962. Reprinted in Concordia Heritage Series, 1982, by Concordia Publishing House with the permission of Augsburg Publishing House, the copyright owner. Page references are to the 1982 reprint.

Concordia: The Lutheran Confessions. Second edition. St. Louis: Concordia Publishing House, 2006.

Craig, William Lane. *Hard Questions, Real Answers*. Wheaton, IL: Crossway Books, 2003.

Cruse, C. F., trans. *Eusebius' Ecclesiastical History: Complete and Unabridged*. New Updated Edition. Peabody, MA: Hendrickson, 1998.

Davids, Peter H. *The First Epistle of Peter*. The New International Commentary on the New Testament. Grand Rapids, MI: William B. Eerdmans, 1990.

Espinosa, Alfonso Odilon. "Apologetics in Pastoral Theology." In *Theologia et Apologia: Essays in Reformation Theology and Its Defense Presented to Rod Rosenblatt*, edited by Adam S. Francisco, Korey D. Maas, and Steven P. Mueller, 317–31. Eugene, OR: Wipf & Stock, 2007. Used by permission of Wipf and Stock Publishers. www.wipfandstock.com.

Espinosa, Alfonso Odilon. "Creation." In *The Lutheran Difference: An Explanation & Comparison of Christian Beliefs*, edited by Edward A. Engelbrecht, 119–52. St. Louis: Concordia Publishing House, 2010.

Espinosa, Alfonso Odilon. *Faith That Sees through the Culture*. St. Louis: Concordia Publishing House, 2018.

Fee, Gordon D. *The First Epistle to the Corinthians*. Rev. ed. The New International Commentary on the New Testament. Grand Rapids, MI: William B. Eerdmans, 2014.

Gurney, Robert J. M. *Six-Day Creation: Does It Matter What You Believe?* Leominster, UK: Day One, 2007. www.dayone.co.uk.

Harari, Yuval Noah. *21 Lessons for the 21st Century*. Spiegel & Grau Trade Paperback Edition. New York: Spiegel & Grau, 2019.

Hauerwas, Stanley, and William H. Willimon. *Where Resident Aliens Live: Exercises for Christian Practice*. Nashville, TN: Abingdon Press, 1996. Used by permission. All rights reserved.

Huchingson, James E., comp. *Religion and the Natural Sciences: The Range of Engagement*. Fort Worth, TX: Harcourt Brace College Publishers, 1993. Used by permission of Wipf and Stock Publishers. www.wipfandstock.com.

Johnson, Phillip Max. "Exposed by the Light: Confessing Our Sin and Naming Our Sins." *Lutheran Forum* (Fall 1997): 15–17.

Keller, Timothy. *Counterfeit Gods: The Empty Promises of Money, Sex, and Power, and the Only Hope That Matters*. New York: Dutton, 2009.

Keller, Timothy. *Making Sense of God: An Invitation to the Skeptical*. New York: Viking, 2016.

Keller, Timothy. *The Reason for God: Belief in an Age of Skepticism*. New York: Riverhead Books, 2009.

Lenski, R. C. H. *The Interpretation of St. Paul's First and Second Epistles to the*

Corinthians. Minneapolis: Augsburg, 1963.

Lenski, R. C. H. *The Interpretation of the Acts of the Apostles*. Minneapolis: Augsburg, 1961.

Lenski, R. C. H. *The Interpretation of the Epistles of St. Peter, St. John and St. Jude*. Minneapolis: Augsburg, 1966.

Lewis, C. S. *Mere Christianity: A Revised and Amplified Edition, with a New Introduction, of the Three Books, Broadcast Talks, Christian Behaviour, and Beyond Personality*. New York: HarperCollins, 2001. MERE CHRISTIANITY by CS Lewis © copyright CS Lewis Pte Ltd 1942, 1943, 1944, 1952.

Lewis, C. S. *The Problem of Pain*. Macmillan Paperback Edition. New York: Macmillan, 1962. THE PROBLEM OF PAIN by CS Lewis © copyright CS Lewis Pte Ltd 1940.

Lindberg, David C., and Ronald L. Numbers, eds. *God and Nature: Historical Essays on the Encounter between Christianity and Science*. Berkeley, CA: University of California Press, 1986.

Lockwood, Gregory J. *1 Corinthians*. Concordia Commentary. St. Louis: Concordia Publishing House, 2000.

Luther, Martin. *Career of the Reformer: I*. Edited by Harold J. Grimm and Helmut T. Lehmann. American Edition. Vol. 31. Luther's Works. Philadelphia: Fortress Press, 1957.

Luther, Martin. *Lectures on Galatians 1535 Chapters 1–4*. Edited by Jaroslav Pelikan and Walter A Hansen. American Edition. Vol. 26. Luther's Works. St. Louis: Concordia Publishing House, 1963.

Luther, Martin. *Luther's Small Catechism with Explanation*. St. Louis: Concordia Publishing House, 1986, 2017.

Luther, Martin. *The Catholic Epistles*. Edited by Jaroslav Pelikan and Walter A Hansen. American Edition. Vol. 30. Luther's Works. St. Louis: Concordia Publishing House, 1967.

Luther, Martin. *What Luther Says: A Practical In-Home Anthology for the Active Christian*. Compiled by Ewald M. Plass. St. Louis: Concordia Publishing House, 1959.

Luther, Martin. *Word and Sacrament: III*. Edited by Robert H. Fischer and Helmut T. Lehmann. American Edition. Vol. 37. Luther's Works. Philadelphia: Fortress Press, 1961.

MacKay, Donald M. *The Clockwork Image: A Christian Perspective on Science*. Christian Classics Series. Leicester, UK: InterVarsity Press, 1997.

Marshall, Ronald F. "Salvation within Our Reach." *Lutheran Forum* (Fall 1997): 18–21.

Martin, Francis, ed. *Acts*. Ancient Christian Commentary on Scripture, New Testament V. Downers Grove, IL: InterVarsity Press, 2006.

Marty, Martin E. "Articles of War, Articles of Peace: Christianity and Culture." In *Christ and Culture in Dialogue: Constructive Themes and Practical Applications*, edited by Angus J. L. Menuge, 57. St. Louis: Concordia Academic Press, 1999.

McGrath, Alister E. *A Fine-Tuned Universe: The Quest for God in Science and Theology*. Gifford Lectures, 2009. Louisville, KY: Westminster John Knox Press, 2009.

McGrath, Alister E. *Intellectuals Don't Need God & Other Modern Myths: Building Bridges to Faith through Apologetics*. Grand Rapids, MI: Zondervan, 1993. Used by permission of Zondervan. www.zondervan.com.

McGrath, Alister E., and Joanna Collicutt McGrath. *The Dawkins Delusion? Atheist Fundamentalism and the Denial of the Divine*. London: SPCK, 2007. Used by permission of SPCK/IVP. spckpublishing.co.uk/.

Nelson, Paul, and John Mark Reynolds. "Young Earth Creationism." In *Three Views on Creation and Evolution*, edited by J. P. Moreland and John Mark Reynolds, 41–102. Counterpoints. Grand Rapids, MI: Zondervan, 1999. Used by permission of Zondervan. www.zondervan.com.

Petersen, Jim. *Living Proof*. Colorado Springs, CO: NavPress, 1989.

Schaeffer, Francis A. *How Should We Then Live? The Rise and Decline of Western Thought and Culture*. Crossway Books Paperback. Westchester, IL: Crossway Books, 1983.

Schlossberg, Herbert. *Idols for Destruction: The Conflict of Christian Faith and American Culture*. Wheaton, IL: Crossway Books, 1993.

Sproul, R. C., John H. Gerstner, and Arthur Lindsley. *Classical Apologetics: A Rational Defense of the Christian Faith and a Critique of Presuppositional Apologetics*. Grand Rapids, MI: Zondervan, 1984.

Used by permission of Zondervan. www.zondervan.com.

Stott, John R. W. *The Spirit, the Church, and the World: The Message of Acts.* Downers Grove, IL: InterVarsity Press, 1990.

The Lutheran Study Bible. St. Louis: Concordia Publishing House, 2009.

Thompson, Tracy. *The Beast: A Reckoning with Depression.* New York: G. P. Putnam's Sons, 1995. Copyright © by Tracy Thompson. Reprinted by permission of Beth Vesel Literary Agency.

Tocqueville, Alexis de. *Democracy in America.* Abridged by Sanford Kessler. Translated by Stephen D. Grant. Indianapolis: Hackett, 2000. Reprinted by permission of Hackett Publishing Company, Inc. All rights reserved.

TOPICAL INDEX

SCRIPTURAL INDEX